The
WEALTH
DECISION

The
WEALTH
DECISION

10 Simple Steps to Achieve Financial Freedom and Build Generational Wealth

....

DOMINIQUE BROADWAY

SIMON ELEMENT

New York   London   Toronto   Sydney   New Delhi

SIMON
ELEMENT

An Imprint of Simon & Schuster, Inc.
1230 Avenue of the Americas
New York, NY 10020

First Simon Element hardcover edition May 2023

SIMON ELEMENT is a trademark of Simon & Schuster, Inc.

For information about special discounts for bulk purchases, please contact Simon & Schuster Special Sales at 1-866-506-1949 or business@simonandschuster.com.

The Simon & Schuster Speakers Bureau can bring authors to your live event. For more information or to book an event, contact the Simon & Schuster Speakers Bureau at 1-866-248-3049 or visit our website at www.simonspeakers.com.

Manufactured in the United States of America

10 9 8 7 6 5 4 3 2 1

Library of Congress Cataloging-in-Publication Data has been applied for.

ISBN 978-1-6680-0836-2
ISBN 978-1-6680-0838-6 (ebook)

THIS BOOK IS DEDICATED TO . . .

My parents, Beverly and Kevin, who always believed
and supported all of my "crazy" ideas.

My baby sister, Bvlgari, who should really be the big sister,
who keeps me organized and believes in everything I do!

My grandparents John and Bernice, who have always been
my biggest supporters in every aspect of my life.

My beautiful daughters, Dawsyn and Demi. Thank you for choosing
me as your mom and bringing joy to my life every day.

CONTENTS

CONTENTS

INTRODUCTION

June 2011

I know what I want, and it's not this. I'm done worrying about bills and obsessing over money. I'm tired of being too scared to open the mail or pick up the phone because of what I owe . . . which is money to everyone. I've spent one too many months scared to leave the house because it'll cost too much. I'm sick and tired of money making me feel sick and tired. I'm done just trying to survive.

No, what I want is big, beautiful, grand, and wealthy. Black people, women, mothers, we deserve financial freedom, too. I'm going to get it for myself and I'm not going to stop working until I've taught every last person how to do the same. One day, my kids will never have to worry about money because I'll have created generational wealth. Fresh-squeezed orange juice will be in my hand as I walk from my bedroom to my office, ready for my first meeting of the day. I'm the CEO. I'll look out from my home with a view, one of many that I own, purchased with my own dollars, and look at nothing but water as far as the eye can see. If someone I love falls on hard times, I'll be there to make sure money isn't an issue. I'll give generously to my community, circulating my money every chance I get. When I want to travel the world and experience every drop out of life, I can. My legacy will be a wealthy one that inspires other people. Financial confidence isn't just for the rich and famous; it's for all of us. Today I decide to be wealthy so that financial confidence is a given for my future children and for every person that looks like me. Mindset got me into this mess and mindset will get me out.

....

When I was a kid, my mom would drive me past mansions in a nearby Potomac, Maryland, neighborhood so I could see how rich people lived. My dad was in prison, and my mom was single-parenting. She'd recently filed for bankruptcy, but she didn't tell me. It was important to her that she not rob me of the opportunity to understand what I could aspire to, even if she couldn't provide it.

Eventually, I did all the right things that would help me live like the rich people—I worked hard throughout school, attending public schools and private schools with the help of my grandparents. I went on to Bowie State University, then to University of Maryland Global Campus. My mom was instrumental in ensuring that I had good schooling, which resulted in a few fancy degrees and a career in finance.

Yet I still managed to end up flat broke. I had debt collectors ringing my phone off the damn hook. They're not allowed to threaten, but they would say things like "If you can't pay this, we're going to take legal action." To me that's a threat, and it's scary. The calls would start at 9 a.m. and constantly blow up my phone from then on. All these years later, I *still* don't answer my phone if I don't know the number. Whether the calls were about my expired warranty, my late condo association fees, my credit cards, or news that my car was about to be repossessed, the phone rang until late into the evening.

I was lying under a pile of rubble and did not see an easy way out. But I managed to turn my total financial ruin around in a year. I became a millionaire in three. Now I'm writing this book, overseeing a multimillion-dollar company, and teaching personal finance and wealth building to people just like you. It may seem like all of this happened quickly, but in reality it was a long time coming when I consider the overall trajectory of my life.

I saw how many of my childhood experiences shaped the emotions that led me to that place of financial ruin.

I had buried my head in the sand, refusing to talk about my struggles, because when I was growing up, we never talked about the bad stuff. Instead we just dreamed for a rich future. I was shielded from the very real struggles happening all around me, like the financial implication of my father being in jail and my mother working to support us but facing bankruptcy. I didn't know that it was totally normal to hit hard times. Until going broke, which almost broke me, I wasn't willing to look at *why* I got there and what I would do differently to never end up there again.

I had to go back before I could move forward.

When I came to the edge of losing everything, that was the turning point in understanding what I really wanted and what it would *really take* to be the first millionaire in my family.

It all started with my decision to prioritize wealth. Let's talk about this term *wealth*, though, because it means different things to different people (which is perfectly fine!). Some of you might attach a hard number to the definition of wealth, like becoming a multimillionaire, while others might attach a feeling to it, like freedom. Some people might want to buy a home, while someone else might want to spend their life traveling the world. Some might envision millions and millions, while someone else cares only about their children's education. Every definition of wealth is different and unique. No matter how you define it, wealth occurs when you control money, not the other way around.

Here's the thing: there's no one money move that's going to lead you to wealth whether you're broke right now, doing all right, or kinda killing it. **Instead, there's *a series of important steps* that will get you there. It starts with one, single decision to *be* wealthy, and it's followed by ten important steps that will empower you to attain your financial goals.**

Owning—and committing—to the fact that you want to be wealthy is a life-altering decision and where your series of steps to get there begins. You don't have to change everything all at once, but you do have to make one important choice at a time. Start immediately, because the best time to tackle your finances is last year. The next-best time is today—right now. By picking up this book, you've made the single most important decision on your way to a life of financial confidence . . . You've decided to begin. And that alone is *huge*. We all have important moments that change our financial destiny, and though they may seem small in hindsight, they create a giant ripple that shifts your future into a new possibility.

It can be hard—impossible even—to imagine a life of wealth when everything around you feels crappy or less-than. This isn't your fault. Our financial systems are set up in such a way that the information on how to get wealthy stays within the walls of certain rooms. Not to mention that large swaths of wealth often pass from one family to the next, creating ongoing inequality. But you've arrived here because you want to talk about money, and because you've dared to dream what might be possible once you do.

. . . And let me tell you, it's going to blow your mind.

You might lack wealth now, but that's not a life sentence. It's a moment in time, and before you know it, you'll be through this book and on your way to a different reality altogether.

No matter what your relationship with money looks like today—tortuous, complicated, neutral, or elated—I'm going to spend these pages giving you exactly what you need to level up. I don't care if you're broke or if you've got Benjamins falling from your pockets. Together we're going to redefine financial freedom and generational wealth and start living it today.

I'm going to make wealth accessible to you.

I wouldn't be here writing this for you, as a self-made multimillionaire, if I hadn't made the choice to turn around my situation when I was struggling financially. At the time, it wasn't that easy. Deciding to prioritize wealth by enlisting help felt like someone asking me to jump off the Empire State Building into a foam pit. However, that decision to shift my mindset allowed me to come clean about my debts and begin a series of financial steps—like defining my dream lifestyle, acting like the CEO of my finances every day, and following a microwave method for tackling the smallest debts first—that were a gateway to wealth. Had I not done these things, I'd still be treading water in Washington, DC, hiding my problems, and making just enough to keep collectors off my back—feeling utterly handcuffed to the realities of my financial circumstances.

But instead, I'm living a truly wealthy life. As I write this, I'm eating a meal that our family cook prepared. As I take my seat in front of my computer to begin working, the Intracoastal Waterway in Miami glimmers like a bright diamond in the floor-to-ceiling windows behind me. I can't believe the magic that I'm living.

I take heart knowing that my young daughters have a secure financial future because I have been investing for them since they were born, and each will have over a million dollars in her name by the time she turns eighteen. As I sit at this desk breastfeeding my new daughter, while leading a call with my team about the business that will reach eight figures in a few months, I feel complete *freedom*. I know—because I've been to the depths of financial hardship and have built my way back—that you can join me here in a life that feels like financial freedom *to you*. It doesn't require having rich parents, an Ivy League education, endless hours in the day, a brilliant idea, or money in the bank.

I know that financial advice can feel unrelatable and out of touch, especially when you're swimming in stress. How are you supposed to know what to do next? Or where to start? Or where to put money? Or how to even *make* money? Or how to have your money make money? Figuring out who to listen to, what to read, and where to go can make you freeze and freak out. This book is a plan to change that.

You can trust that I'm the person who can both hold your hand and coach you with authority. I built my career as a licensed financial planner and have worked at major, corporate brokerage firms like UBS and Edelman. My bachelor's *and* my master's degrees are in business and finance. I like viral social media posts about money as much as the next person, but I prefer that you listen to people like me who have financial expertise and a lengthy history of studying, practicing, and teaching personal finance. We'll tell you what's really up. I plan to share all the modern platforms, learnings, and strategies that you won't find from your friend's parents' financial advisor. Stale financial advice doesn't cut it anymore—the world is moving too fast.

Whatever your financial reality right now—whether you're broke or boundless—I've designed this book as a series of steps to give every person the chance to experience wealth. I mean *every single person*. No matter how far behind you feel, no matter how much you have saved, no matter if you have all the degrees or none of them. Whether you have countless investments or don't even know what an investment is—this book is for you. I don't care what you look like or where you come from: I'm going to give you the chance to experience true financial freedom.

With access to the information in this book, my renowned expertise, unlimited possibilities to create income, and my road map for exactly what to do, you'll see your wealthy future appear one decision at a time and make sure it stays there not just for the present moment, but also for future generations. That's why this book is broken down into the ten steps you need to build generational wealth, with countless small choices in between that will ensure you're headed in the right direction.

First, we'll explore your mindsets around money. We'll assess where they came from, how to shift the ones that aren't helping you, and how to start thinking differently about your future. The next series of steps will lay the foundation for your financial success, like how to tackle your debt monster and spend your way to wealth (yes, *spend*!). We'll make our way to steps that lay bare the tricks of really wealthy people, like creating multiple revenue streams and protecting your assets so that your wealth lasts for generations.

Tapping into why you've opened this book will give you momentum and purpose on this wealth-building journey. Here are some questions to ponder before we dive in. Go ahead and get out a pen and write down some answers that come up for you. (Or visit the QR code at the back of this book, which directs you to thewealthdecision.co, to work with an online version of these questions. Keep that QR code close, because you'll be using it to access digital versions of all the questions, prompts, worksheets, and resources you'll find in each chapter.) **The phone icon below is your visual reminder to visit the QR code.**

- What do you want people to say about you when you're gone?

- How do you want to make people feel?

- If your day could be about creating one outcome, emotion, or benefit for people, what would it be and who are those people?

- Imagine you have the wealth you desire. What is that wealth helping you do that is in service to others?

- If you had all the time in the world to focus on one issue, one group of people that you care about, one cause, or one change, what would it be?

You've already made the most important decision to get started and **prioritize your wealth**, so let's jump right into the rest.

CHAPTER 1

Take Back the Power

TO TAKE BACK THE POWER . . .

- Assess your relationship with money.
- Talk about money.
- Know *why* you don't know.

Seven years ago, my grandfather and I sat at my kitchen table surrounded by a pile of ripped-open envelopes. We placed a stack of folded bills in the middle of the table, and opened a notebook with a list of money owed. Each notice threatened to sink me further into debt. The situation was a beast, a financial monster to whom I had handed over every ounce of my power. Money controlled my life, not me. My grandfather, who was the chief of information technology (IT) for the Department of Defense and had no formal financial training, sat right next to me in the kitchen as we reviewed each debt, determined which were the most damning, prioritized which needed immediate attention, and rehearsed what to say to debt collectors. He provided what I needed most—nonjudgmental support—and what I plan to give you throughout this book.

The year before this kitchen-table moment had been terrible, but it was supposed to be my rocket ship. After more than six years working for elite financial institutions and consulting for the very rich on how to manage their money, I finally took the leap toward seeing my own dreams come true. See, I'd spent one too many meetings with people who looked nothing like me, giving them the absolute best financial advice that money could buy. It felt like heartless work—these people didn't need me. They had enough money for their great-great-great-grandchildren's children. My last corporate job was working directly with the owner of a firm who was preparing me to take over his business. I created clients' financial plans, made investments for those plans, met with clients, and made changes to their investment portfolios. But I always felt like I was supposed to do something else, something different. There were so many people who had never had access to the kind of knowledge and conversations that I was having in those rooms, and I wanted to change that.

Over the course of a few years, I made a vow to create a business that gave access to financial expertise to people who had traditionally been kept out of those rooms—the rooms I'd fought to be in and where I was often the only Black woman for miles. I was going to demystify personal finance for people, and, in the process, take charge of my own career. I could pay myself what I deserved, and I could be deliberate about how I spent my days. I kept my dreams to myself for a year while I saved $50,000 as a cushion and I prepared to go full-time with my business. Then I transitioned out of the corporate world.

For the first year of running my business, every day I spent away from the safety net of full-time employment, I told myself: *It's going to get better.* As I watched my savings dwindle, my credit card balance expand, and my credit score plummet, I believed it *had* to improve. It couldn't keep going this way, because *I* couldn't go broke. I had experience. I had expertise. I was running a business teaching first-generation adults how to build generational wealth . . . This couldn't be happening to me.

Except that it was, and within a year of quitting my corporate job, I was out of runway because my expenses were higher than my self-employed income. I cut back on everything. There was no more eating out, not even a quick coffee run. I cooked almost every meal at home. I didn't go on vacation. I didn't buy new clothes or get my nails done. But I still blew through my savings paying my mortgage because I simply wasn't making enough money from my own business. Before I knew it, I was behind on my car note, my homeowner association fees, my mortgage payment, my credit card bill, and my utilities because I kept thinking, *Next month my business will bring in more money, and I'll be fine.*

I was a licensed financial planner who was going broke. Feeling like an imposter doesn't even begin to explain it. My days were shrouded in shame and embarrassment, and the idea of admitting to *anyone* what was going on financially was enough to sink me further into despair.

Was my old boss right? On the day I gave my notice he said, "You'll never make money helping people who don't have money." Did he know something that I didn't? It's not like he was some old, rich white dude. He was a Black man to whom I looked up and whose opinion I respected, but when he made that comment, I believed that he was wrong. Plus, I was a hella saver, and there's no way *I* could be someone who let their finances get out of control. While I was confident I would prove him wrong eventually, I didn't know it would have to get worse before it got better.

I quit my job to start my own business helping others make money, but because I was putting all of my own resources into my business and wasn't making enough, I ended up in debt. I was helping everyone else excel financially, but I was drowning. I buried my head in the sand, wouldn't pick up calls from numbers I didn't recognize, and refused to open my mail. It was always a bill or a debt collector, and I didn't want to face either one. I didn't get it. I wasn't spending lavishly and I had devoted my life's work to getting financial information to the people who needed it. Didn't my intention, education, and certifications in this very industry safeguard me from making the same mistakes I warned my clients and students against?

The cause of my financial troubles is superclear to me now. I wasn't charging clients enough money for my services, so my income never exceeded my expenses. But I refused to acknowledge that fact. As it turns out, nothing can save us from financial troubles when we're choosing to do nothing about them and giving money all of our power by letting it rule our emotions.

The debt and stress were controlling every waking moment of my life. Not only did my finances feel out of control, but my entire existence felt that way, too. My troubles came to a head one day after long hours of hustling to make my ends meet. Someone came to my door, and when I opened it, I got served. They handed me a big ol' envelope full of documents saying that my condo association was suing me for unpaid condo fees and placing a lien on my property. A lien isn't a good thing. It's a legal claim on an asset granted by the courts saying it can be repossessed or used as collateral to repay a debt. This meant that I either couldn't sell the house without paying them, or proceeds would go to them after my mortgage was paid off if I did manage to sell it. On top of the money that I owed the association for unpaid dues, I would also have to pay ongoing late fees and superhigh lawyer fees. As I stood there flipping through each document, I was shaking. I couldn't handle this debt any longer. Every money problem seemed like it created ten more. It was then that **I made one decision that altered the course of my financial future** and the future of my two children, too:

I decided to prioritize *my* wealth, which meant putting my well-being first by creating financial stability. I couldn't keep making other people's wealth a priority over my own or bury my head in the sand any longer. I needed a plan.

The first step was talking to my mom—a bigger deal than you might imagine. I didn't want to admit that I was swimming in debt, but in retrospect, I'm so glad I did. When I came clean to my mom, who, since those hard days when she would drive me around the fancy homes, owned a company that helped people who were behind on their mortgages, I learned something I hadn't known. In the years after my dad was released from prison, she had filed for bankruptcy. If you're not familiar with the specifics, bankruptcy is a petition that individuals or businesses can file with the courts when they're unable to pay their debts, so that they're erased. These days, it requires that you liquidate your assets to pay off your debts or follow a payment plan to pay them back.[1] Bankruptcy is normally a last resort for people because it stays on your credit report, making it harder to get loans, credit cards, or mortgages in the future. My mom shared the fear *she* felt about having to file for bankruptcy and how she worked her way back.

My mom taught me that really smart people go through financial hardships, too. But when this is happening to you, you feel like you're the only one. With her reassurance that I wasn't the first person to hit a rough patch like this (and I wouldn't be the last), I took my troubles to my grandfather, who, without judgment, helped me open up each piece of mail and write down every last amount that I owed and to whom. And that's what we did, bill by bill, until I had a plan.

The plan in that first year was simply to get out of debt. I negotiated with creditors to create payment schedules for my debts, sometimes paying as little as fifty bucks a month because that's all that I could afford. I took on a consulting job at a nonprofit that hosted financial literacy camps for kids. I oversaw the programming, designing the events and coordinating speakers. In theory I should have loved this work, but the environment wasn't very welcoming.

The office was in the basement of the owner's home, which felt cold, empty, and depressing. I knew that each hour I was spending there was not being spent in my business.

While I was grateful for the income, I absolutely loathed having to keep this gig for extra money. Each morning I'd pull up to work in a panic, wondering how I'd get through the day. I kept showing up for work that I hated so I wouldn't have to lose my house or shut down my new business. I had to liquidate every investment I had because I needed the money. Eventually this stability of recurring, guaranteed income from my consulting job gave way to more energizing decisions, step by step, like selling my home on my own terms, taking a business trip when I needed to, or buying a drink *not* during happy hour. As my foundation firmed up, I was able to take on more financial risk, such as putting money into endeavors that would make me more money (you'll learn about those in chapter 9), investing in my favorite companies, geeking out on crypto, and even teaching people how to day-trade.

I share my past with you so that you understand that I've been there. I haven't just helped tens of thousands of people step into a path of wealth, but I've also done it for myself, too. But the moment I decided to prioritize wealth, creating financial freedom as a path to my well-being and facing every last reality of my debt, was a crucial one because it was then that my agency returned. This meant that I had options. When you *decide to take back the power* that money has over your life, you begin to build wealth. Money no longer controls you. The number in your bank account no longer determines if you're happy or sad, or if you're stressed or relaxed. It's no longer running your life because you are implementing steps that put *you* in control. Not the other way around. Most important, no longer do you have to live with a massive monster that is getting scarier by the day. Together we're going to turn this into an adventure with *you* in the driver's seat.

Assess Your Relationship with Money

The wealth decision requires that you face where you're at, and you don't need to be like me and be served papers over a lawsuit to do that. As we journey through your wealth-building, knowing where you're starting from will help you get to where you want to be. Now be honest, y'all: I want you to consider how you're really doing when it comes to the relationship with your personal finances. We can't change the stuff we're ignoring. Here are a few questions that can help you assess things realistically, which you can also find at the QR code in the back of the book:

- On a scale of 1–10, with 1 being the worst and 10 the best: how do you feel about your relationship to money?

  1 2 3 4 5 6 7 8 9 10

- Why do you feel that way?

  _____

  _____

- If you ranked yourself less than a 10, what area of your finances do you avoid?

  _____

  _____

- Do you avoid looking at your bank statements because of what numbers might be there? **YES** or **NO**
- Do you feel anxious every time you log in to your credit card account? **YES** or **NO**
- Do you leave mail unopened because you don't want to deal with the bills? **YES** or **NO**

- Do you see the material things that other people have and feel unworthy? **YES** or **NO**
- Do you get embarrassed when you don't know a financial term and keep the question to yourself? **YES** or **NO**
- Do you avoid conversations about money with your partner, family, or friends? **YES** or **NO**

Your answers are a starting point for knowing what needs your attention. I find that the areas that we're the least confident about when it comes to our finances, we typically avoid, which damages our relationship to money—whether it's debts, spending plans, investing, or retirement planning. It's like any other relationship: every aspect of a friendship, marriage, or familial connection won't be perfect all the time. But the more work you put into the not-so-great areas of those relationships, the better the entire relationship gets. With money, the areas you're avoiding are the same ones that serve as the building blocks that will help you make major gains in your wealth-building journey. Luckily, we're going to do that together instead of turning a blind eye and letting your problems spiral out of control.

If you ignore your relationship to money, you're giving it all of the power. I know when you don't have money, it feels like money is some grand ruler over the happiness of your days, but that's part of the power we're going to decide to retrieve in this chapter. Money is gratitude we hand over for things that we like, love, and need. It's also gratitude we produce for our time, knowledge, products, and service. It's just the circulation of energy.

This is why you must take your energy out of stressing about money or debt and use it for other purposes instead. It's as simple as that. It's important to understand that if you put too much emphasis on money, you're letting the amount of money in your bank account determine how you feel that day. When you do this, money decides how you live your life and what you're worth, instead of realizing *you* get to decide. That control is really important so you can turn your dreams into a financial reality.

Not sure if you've given your power away? Circle any of these statements that you believe about *money*:

- Money makes me a better person.
- Money brings happiness.
- Money makes me more worthy.
- Money is a finite resource.
- Money is hard to come by.
- Money causes problems.
- Money is evil.
- Money decides my fate.

These myths about money are common, so it's normal if you circled a few or all of them. But we're going to shatter them throughout this book by understanding what it takes to create financial freedom.

To evict fear from your wallet, see money as the naked old guy standing onstage unable to find his clothes. If you answered *yes* to any of the questions above, you're giving your money too much power. Handling your finances can be fun and exciting, but it will never feel that way if your fear about what's happening (or *could* happen) runs the show. Look, because money is energy—and it's everywhere—there are plenty of opportunities to lose your compass when it comes to getting your mind right about your finances. Before we dig into your specific financial realities in the coming chapters, you've got to put yourself back in the power position, starting with your conversations about money.

Engage in a Conversation about Money to Take Your Power Back

The first and most important way to take back your power with money is to start talking about it—good and/or bad. If I yelled, "Let's talk about sex," people would turn their heads to see who said it, with curiosity and intrigue on their faces. But if I yelled, "Let's talk about money," people wouldn't respond because they'd be too busy hiding and avoiding the conversation altogether. I can say, based on a career spent talking about money, that most people are raised *not* to talk about it. We don't share how much we make, and we definitely don't share if we are in any financial trouble. Because money is a taboo topic, we end up in deep holes. As with anything that brings shame or fear, if you can just start talking about it, you disempower those feelings and gather strength to deal with the situation.

My client Kimberly transformed her wealth by starting with the small act of talking about her finances. She worked for the federal government, and had a great income, but was petrified to talk about her finances or even look at her bank accounts. She was always scared that there wouldn't be enough or that she might have overdrafted. When she was growing up, money wasn't something Kimberly talked about in her home, and she'd often overhear her parents arguing about it. Those feelings stayed with her. The topic of money continued to make her upset, anxious, and scared even when she was no longer under her parents' roof.

When Kimberly and I worked together, that gradually started to change. At first she said that even coming to our meetings gave her anxiety, even though I was there to help. Over time, she got comfortable looking at her money and talking about it with me and those closest to her. This allowed her to take back her power, get clear with the state of her finances, and start making decisions that would build her wealth, like investing her money in the stock market and putting some of her money into real estate.

I get Kimberly's resistance. I was so scared to tell anyone about my financial hardship during the year I started my business, even though I made a living talking to others about money. *And* I was fortunate to have been raised in a family that talked about money. My mom taught me—and made sure that I understood—what it really took to run a household financially. My grandparents also had financial conversations with me about the "spenders and savers" in life. They emphasized how, as a family, we were to support one another in our time of need. That's exactly what they did when I hit my financial rock bottom, which made me regret how long I'd avoided being honest with them when they could have helped.

In other words, even under the best circumstances, even if you're in one of the rare families that do talk about money, even if you've been reassured that money is an open topic, it's still difficult to admit hardship. The sooner we ask for guidance, the sooner we can turn things around and start working on the problem before it worsens.

This is why I want you to have a money conversation with a loved one, friend, or family member today. Whether you're experiencing financial stress, or simply wanting to improve where you're at, this conversation is the best way to lift each other up and bring your dreams—and your loved one's dreams—into reality.

Here are two scripts you can use—one if you're in a tough spot and one if you're in a place of positive dreaming—to engage in a conversation about money that helps you take your power back.

MONEY CONVO SCRIPT 1: IF YOU'RE IN A TOUGH SPOT . . .

Ask an open-ended question to someone in your support system:

- What's the roughest financial patch you've ever been through?
- How did you get through it and who did you confide in?
- What types of feelings do you remember experiencing at the time?

Once they've answered or shared stories about their experience, then ask:

- Would you be open to giving me advice on something that I'm currently experiencing?

Respond by saying what you've been going through. Feel free to stay high-level until you feel comfortable. Once you share, follow up with:

- I admire you and how you live your life. Would you be open to sitting down with me to help me solve some of the specifics of my financial challenges right now?

Then commit to a date where you bring everything written down that you're worried about and see what advice they might have. While they're not expected to be a financial expert, having someone with whom you can process your problems out loud is an important first step in deciding to take your power back.

MONEY CONVO SCRIPT 2: WHEN YOU'RE TRYING TO LEAN INTO YOUR FINANCIAL POSSIBILITIES . . .

Ask an open-ended question to someone who has a financial reality that you admire:

- How do you define being wealthy? Is it a number, an achievement, or a feeling?
- What has helped you believe that you could get to where you are today?
- Is there anything that you've done, specifically, that you'd recommend I do to follow in your footsteps?

Once they've answered or shared some stories about their experience, then ask:

- Would you be open to giving me specific advice on how I get from where I am to where I want to be?

Then share with them where you desire to be. Once that happens, follow up with:

- I admire you and what you've created for your life. Would you be open to sitting down with me to help me to dream up what might be possible for my financial future?

Then commit to a date for this follow-up conversation. While this person should not be expected to be a financial expert, having someone to process your dreams out loud is an important first step in deciding to claim power over your financial future.

Know *Why* You Don't Know

Knowledge is power, which is why we place such an important emphasis on education. Why, then, would we not be having any kind of money conversations, much less education, way before our twenties and thirties? My students and clients ask me this all the time (and hell, it's a major reason why I'm writing this book). Wouldn't it be easier to tackle our finances and have a normal and healthy relationship to money, its energy, and conversations around it if we'd been doing it all along? *Of course!* But there's a specific reason that the information about how to make good financial decisions isn't taught when you're young.

Financial institutions profit from you *not* knowing!

Think about it . . . If you don't know what an interest rate is (the proportion of a loan that is charged as interest to the borrower, typically expressed as an annual percentage of the outstanding loan), a bank can make incredible amounts of money off you over your lifetime with a high interest rate. Someone is making money each month you carry a balance. The greater your balance, the more they are making. Or, if you don't know how or why to maintain a good credit score (you will after this book!), a bank will make a fortune from the higher interest rate you have to take on your mortgage. There are hundreds of ways that people make money from your not knowing how financial institutions run their businesses. By ensuring that finance remains "complicated," other people profit.

I hope that *today* you will dive into understanding the basics (or relearning them) and jump enthusiastically into the adventures later in the book, like modern investment strategies and legacy building. I bring this up because we need to make sure that not only are *you* attaining your financial dreams, but also that you become a nonjudgmental educator to someone who needs it.

As you take the steps in this book, like choosing to take your power back—**share what you're learning with someone else who could use support on their financial journey.** That's how we make up for the fact they're not teaching this in schools. That's how we shift the power structures to a more equitable future. And that's how we all support each other in achieving our financial dreams together.

You're nodding your head vigorously and promising me, right? I thought so.

I'm glad you're going to share your knowledge. I'm even more glad that you've decided to reclaim your power around money. It starts with awareness. It starts with assessment. So, while this chapter may not have felt like the warmest, "it'll all be okay" read when it comes to planning your financial future, trust me that we'll get there. I've seen how even the best money and wealth strategies fall apart if you don't shine light on all the wayback places where you've given your power away to money and stayed silent in your financial troubles. In the coming chapters, we're going to move from the important, yet sometimes amorphous, topic of the *energy* you place around money to more concrete topics, starting with assessing your exact situation and how to progress quickly and decidedly toward wealth.

CHAPTER 2

Trace Your Money Origins

TRACE YOUR MONEY ORIGINS BY . . .

- Knowing the six money environments and recognize which ones hold you back.

- Understanding the impact of your money environments.

- Identifying the strong emotions you have around money and shift them.

When I was growing up, I thought I was rich. I paid bills, traveled to the bank, wrote checks, and felt on top of the financial world. Well, sort of. Although I was only eight, I sat with my mom while she wrote out checks. A few years later, when I was in middle school and old enough to have a realistic understanding of money—its value, how we got it, why we used it—my mom and I would sit down every month on her payday and pay the bills together. She'd walk over with her stack of paper bills, and I'd hand her a blue pen and her floral checkbook, each sheet covered in beautiful shades of pink and purple. Bible verses were printed on each check, and I read them aloud before we filled them out. Mom would show me how much money she made that month from her job as an accountant, and then we'd write out a check for rent, the car note, or the utilities bill.

Once all the bills were paid, we'd visit the bank, where I'd fill out a deposit slip with the money Mom made from her side gig selling clothes. Then I'd walk up to the bank teller, my mom standing close, and complete the transaction. Somehow, even paying the bills was a positive experience growing up. I know now that while she loved the ritual with me, she didn't feel quite so positive about money then.

The realities of our financial situation were grim. With Dad incarcerated, we were living on much less than we needed. While I don't know exactly what we couldn't afford in those days because she never let on, Mom went broke many times during the years I was helping her write out those checks. But she didn't break our payday ritual. Luckily for both of us, my grandparents helped here and there to keep us from drowning in debt and to ensure that I went to a good school.

These first experiences were highly educational and mostly positive, and are probably why I decided to make a career out of financial planning in the first place. However, those same experiences also created a false reality that everything was fine, and I had very little insight into how you handle things when your finances go south. My mother chose to hide her struggles from me. So, when I hit difficult times myself, I didn't know that financial challenges were normal and even expected. More important, I had no idea that there are easy-to-follow road maps, not only for overcoming those challenges, but also for building wealth that grows far beyond the ruin.

It's difficult to get there unless you understand your financial origin stories. Where did your relationship with money come from? Your mindset, attitude, and beliefs impact your actions, and they're informed by your ancestry. What your caregivers taught you to believe about money comes from *their* experience, both negative and positive. These ideas about money, which become mindsets, get passed down generation after generation like genetics.

Understanding the root of your relationship with money is the prerequisite to making changes to get beyond it. In the pages that follow, I will help you recognize the money environments you experienced, both from your childhood and your recent past. A money environment is the unique set of circumstances related to your upbringing that informs how you think about finances: the people you're surrounded by, your schooling, who is in and out of your home, the television or music you watched or didn't. Money environments impact how and what you think about money, creating your beliefs. Those money beliefs taken together create your money mindset.

Money environments > money beliefs >
money belief system > money mindset

Before we take a deep dive into the money environments that inform our mindsets around money, I want to first acknowledge something that impacts our ability to have rich money mindsets: inequality. I can't be out here talking about money without addressing the systems and structures that make it harder for some of us to build wealth than others. I don't want you thinking about where your financial mindset originated, beating yourself up about where you came from, and thinking it's all your fault or your mama's fault. It's not. But if you can pay attention to the environments at play— the ones that formed you, that formed your ideas, that formed your beliefs—then you'll be able to see that your initial obstacles to building wealth are not yours. They were pushed on you by racism, sexism, and all the rest of the isms. We were told that because we're a person of color, or a woman, or gay, or disabled, or from a poor background, we don't deserve wealth. And that even though you've been working harder—much harder than some of your peers who don't look like you or who don't come from where you come from—inequality makes you believe you'll never shift some of these patterns.

You will.

I'm proof.

As a Black woman, this frustrates me. I grew up surrounded by kids from other cultures, so I saw how different life could be for each of us. My best friend growing up, Peggy, who is white, provided an early master class on this topic. She lived down the street and we were together all the time. I would always come home reporting on Peggy's every move: *Mom, Peggy did this or Peggy did that.* And Mom always told me, *Dominique, you can't do what Peggy does. Peggy might just show up, but you have to show up a hundred times better because you're a Black girl.* Perfection was required of me. If I left the house, I couldn't have a string of hair out of place. I always had to be dressed to a T. I couldn't have my elbows on the table. I had to speak like a white girl but better.

This mindset still impacts me today. I can't roll into an important meeting in a hoodie with no makeup on and expect to be taken seriously. My TikToks won't go viral if my teeth don't look clean. And don't even get me started on the expertise and multiple degrees it takes to get in those rooms or on those screens. My white peers, however, can do so much less with a tenth of the experience. These realities are embedded into my subconscious, but I am glad I didn't let my mind get the best of me. And I don't want societal inequalities creeping in to deflate how you're thinking about money.

You don't need me going on about racism, sexism, classism, or homophobia because it's more than likely your lived experience. But I do want you to keep them in mind as you work through the more specific money environments we dive into next. Because without acknowledging what was happening all around you, you're not seeing your relationship to money clearly.

Six Money Environments That May Be Holding You Back

In my business teaching people how to build wealth, I've seen it all. There's not an origin story around money—however sad, unbelievable, positive, or out there—that I haven't heard. As humans, we're complicated and messy. So are the people we love, the people who taught us what to believe about money. I share this because sometimes looking back can be hard. You may not want to. You might want to skip right over this "mindset stuff" and get to the chapters on trading and crypto. *Please don't.* I can tell you, having worked with some of the wealthiest people in the country, that when you don't understand *why* you're making decisions, you're bound to make bad ones.

You're going to be making good decisions throughout this book, great ones actually, because you're reading this. You're willing to look at the parts of your story that are uncomfortable to understand how you got here. I promise that once you do, you'll have a solid foundation with which to make better choices. If you've ever tried to get your finances together and that failed, or tried to build wealth only to slide backward, oftentimes examining your first money experiences is one of the missing pieces.

The money environments we grew up in can tell us so much about the choices we're making now, consciously or unconsciously. Here are some of the environments I see the most. Star the ones that most resonate with you.

1. Scam Central

If you grew up around people who believed that nothing is as it seems, and repeating, "If it's too good to be true then it probably is," you've probably felt the impacts of a scam central environment. In this environment, people constantly try to protect themselves from being swindled, taken advantage of, and scammed. Believing everything is a scam can protect someone because they're on high alert.

But it also means that these people miss out on good opportunities because they believe everything and everyone is out to get their money. Once I was sitting with a client who was a year out from retiring and was nervous she wouldn't have enough money because it had been sitting in a money market account, only growing by about 1 percent year after year. I explained that her account could have been over a million dollars if it had been in the stock market, which really upset her. She told me something I hear all the time, that she'd always avoided the stock market because the people around her told her it was a scam.

This is one example of what can happen when someone immediately dismisses everything they can't see and understand. They end up getting left behind. Their wealth, especially. Some of the best wealth-building opportunities come as a result of things we don't immediately understand or easily conceptualize. When I first heard about investing in the stock market, for example, it sounded like gambling to me. I thought the people who told you to invest were scammers just trying to take your money. While the stock market can seem opaque, it is not a scam. It just requires education. Growing up in an environment where everything is a scam causes people to side-eye the very things they need to learn about to grow their wealth.

2. Money Desert

Environments of extreme lack or poor households can create massive shame around money. Maybe your utilities were shut off, you were hungry at school but hiding it, or you couldn't engage in certain conversations—like ones about nannies, exciting vacations, inheriting money, second homes, or two-parent households—because they simply weren't your reality.

I remember working with one gentleman who was the first person in his family ever to make six figures. He'd grown up in a neighborhood and home that never had any money. His family received government assistance and was constantly in survival mode. Once he started making over $250,000 a year, he had a lot of shame around money, based on where he came from. He didn't want to tell anyone and often struggled to "enjoy" the money or make any investment moves, fearing that it would all go away. He finally shifted when he realized how his money desert environment had impacted his mindset, and that in fact his money could be used for more than just survival and bare necessities.

These environments breed a feeling that money is easy to come by and even easier to multiply because no one around you has enough to know. When you grow up never talking about how to accumulate wealth because survival is all that matters, you may internalize the idea that your financial situation will never change. You might believe this is just how the money story is going to be and that wealth is something that only happens for other people, no matter how hard you work. It makes it hard to believe that you deserve and have what it takes to achieve the wealth that you desire. That wealth can be *your* story and that you can change the story for so many people around you.

3. Torrential Rainy Day

If you grew up in an environment where someone was always planning for the worst-case scenario *or* if you had firsthand experience of the impacts of going broke, you can understand why one might go overboard with saving, even keeping gobs of cash in their house *just in case*. I once had a client who lived at home and would save almost 90 percent of her salary . . . in cash. This meant her money was never working for her and it couldn't even keep up with the inflation rate. She was actually losing money every day by saving it for something terrible to happen in the future.

People who are always planning for the worst-case scenarios, but to an extreme, hoard their money. They're so worried about needing it for a rainy day that they can't let go of it. And not just for a rainy day, but for the next great flood. This can create frugal mindsets. Yes, there can be savings, which is great, but there is an opportunity cost to saving beyond what is necessary. In other words, there's less leverage created for more wealth, because all of that wealth is kept away in savings accounts, where it can't grow. But at least it's there if everything does actually fall apart! Growing up in a home where a caregiver is hyper-focused on saving and never spending anything can prevent you from learning how to spend well, giving money a job, and making smart decisions that will multiply your money (which we'll do together).

4. Broke Millionaire

This is the environment ruled by instant gratification. People in this situation spend money before it even comes in, and borrow against money that isn't theirs yet because they can't wait. Money just burns right there in their hands. As soon as they've got it, they have to figure out what they're going to do with it and where to spend it. Broke millionaires breed in an environment that makes it hard to become a millionaire. When I did financial planning for an NFL client, this man would literally try to spend every dollar he made. The only solution at the time was to automatically move it out of his hands and invest it so that he couldn't spend it. When you're acting like this, you can end up being your own enemy because it is impossible for you to build wealth.

Broke millionaires have a hard time picturing the future. *Who cares about six years from now. I'm trying to turn up this Friday!* They don't see the benefit of saving money or investing because they view money as something that should be spent, rather than using it to make more money to build wealth and architect the future. This environment reminds me of that rap song with the lyrics "cash a check, get it right back." Except that if you burn through money as soon as you have it, you may not always get it right back.

5. Ostriching

If ignorance was bliss where you grew up, you might have been in an environment where everyone kept their head in the sand on important financial issues. When the prevailing belief is that money problems will just disappear, and that it's scary to deal with them, you learn to think that addressing them will only make things worse. This was an environment I was creating in my own home when I was ignoring my very real financial troubles in hopes that they would just go away. You don't realize that you actually have the power and knowledge to make things better, and without support or help, your financial struggles metastasize in the darkness. An ostrich environment kicks the bucket down the road and creates a microculture where everyone figures they'll deal with the problems at another time, when they have the capacity to pay it off or wrap their heads around it. Naturally, this rarely happens.

6. Pleasing and Helping

Growing up around people who are generous, kindhearted, and helpful is a beautiful thing. However, like anything, generosity can become extreme, and if the expectation or desire to be generous comes at the cost of one's own well-being, it can create a money environment with negative consequences. This can happen in any household, but it often occurs in first-generation and immigrant households where one family might be doing considerably better financially than its extended families. Guilt often shows up and causes someone to give everything they have to other people at the risk of going broke or unable to build wealth. There *is* such a thing as being *too* generous if you're trying to build wealth, which you'll learn from reading about my client Felicia in a few pages.

These aren't the only financial environments that exist, but they're the common ones. Understanding which one you grew up in, and how you might have spent your formidable years soaking up information that informed your belief system around wealth, is a powerful step in becoming wealthy.

The Impact of Your Money Environments

The only negative memories I have around money come from the period after my dad got out of prison, and the conversations I overheard around that time. My mom would argue with him about paying child support and supporting me financially now that he was out. When he would get behind on the support he was paying, they'd get into fights about that. I truly didn't understand why my dad would be so cheap and not share his money with us.

But when I get really honest, many of the money environments I named are the very ones that showed up in my own life—not always at the same time, but in hindsight, they were definitely there. I was forced to examine them to understand how I ended up in this degree of financial trouble.

When I was a kid, my mom thought *everything* was a scam. We couldn't have the dang Boy Scouts knocking on our door about popcorn without her wondering what kind of trouble they were trying to get us into. I don't blame her. She was risk-averse because she was trying to get by on a single income while raising me. She didn't have a choice but to be cautious and imagine the worst possible financial scenario. That's what kept us safe.

But as a result, I grew up thinking everything was a scam, too. When my business was just taking off, I side-eyed opportunities if I didn't readily recognize the company or person that was approaching me. I couldn't help it. It was ingrained in me from childhood that it all might be a cover-up to swindle me.

My mom remarried when I was in high school, and I had a first-row look into another environment—the broke millionaire. It didn't impact me much at first, until I saw some of the behaviors in a person I loved and relied on the most. A few years ago, I shared with my stepfather, Marvin, that I wanted to write a book soon. Sadly, Marvin died before he could see this dream come to life, but he told me, "Let me write the chapter on how to *not* become a millionaire and then go broke." I promised I'd let him. My stepfather lived life like money was burning a hole in his pocket. As his income increased, his lifestyle would immediately expand. He would come home with a new Range Rover sitting on twenty-two-inch rims and not long after, he'd crash that Range Rover and not have the money to fix it. While I don't know the exact ways Marvin was mishandling money, he was always broke and borrowing money despite a big ol' income. I saw that and was petrified that if I increased my lifestyle, I would become him.

That's why it was like pulling nails for my partner at the time to get me to move into a new, much nicer place where I'd have my own office, room for our growing family, and a view that inspires me. I was so scared that the money that gave me security now would go away and I would come crashing down. I'd be re-creating my stepfather's pattern in my own life. So, I save . . . way more than is recommended. Even my own chief financial officer (CFO) has commented about how my lifestyle and spending have not evolved with the success of my business. It's true. Full disclosure: I save a greater percentage of my income than I might tell someone else to save, but I manage my mindset in such a way that it doesn't interfere with my wealth-building journey.

As I've said, I went broke in my twenties because I was ostriching, burying my head in the sand because I'd learned that I couldn't or shouldn't talk about my struggles and ask for help. Not only was I a financial planner, but I'd been taught about money from such a young age. I had no right to screw this up. The shame nearly overwhelmed me.

This is what happens. You experience something, and those experiences create a ripple effect that impacts your life in various ways. So, to begin making better decisions around wealth, you have to first understand the money environments and experiences that might be impacting you negatively today. The beliefs holding you back might have served you as a kid, or a younger version of yourself with different circumstances, but it's time to change them.

Identify Those Strong Emotions

When my partner at the time told me that we should move homes now that I was making more money—like a lot more—I had a *strong* emotion. Very strong. We were living in a two-bedroom apartment that was absolutely beautiful, with floor-to-ceiling windows. But we were working out of our living room, which made running a business pretty difficult if the kids were asleep and I had to teach a class. It felt like we were all living on top of each other. I protested his suggestion to move into a two-floor, multimillion-dollar condo on the beach, which would allow each of us to have our own office, a car elevator, and a serviced beach and pool. I thought he was dead wrong to even suggest it, even though it was a reasonable percentage of our income to spend on housing (less than 20 percent). I was perfectly happy in our little apartment and didn't see the need for an upgrade. It was foolish to even look at a place that cost as much as the ones he was showing me. I didn't care if our business was on a rocket ship to the moon. What if the moon disappears? What if the rocket ship breaks? I was not moving.

Strong emotions can be an immediate reaction to childhood environments or past hardships. My emotions came from not wanting to die without a dollar to my name, like my stepdad. However, my partner expressed in four-hour-long conversations that I deserved everything I worked for and that I should enjoy it. He reminded me that I would never allow myself to end up like my stepfather, so it was an unnecessary worry. Once I saw that he was right, I got excited.

Trust me when I say that life got so much better when we upgraded our space. Our business became even more successful because I was inspired, healthy, and happy in our new home. I always envisioned having a nanny, a chef, and a housekeeper, and we had them. This allowed me the space and time to dream bigger in my business and helped elevate my mood every day. That, in turn, allowed me to focus on my vision for helping everyone become financially confident. My beliefs shifted and for the first time, I felt like I had "made it" and that I deserved to be there.

My beliefs were upgraded along with my environment.

I've been working on understanding my own experiences with money, and coaching others formally and informally for decades. It's a part of the work when you're dealing with money. Even *I* have strong emotions that still pop up. The point isn't that you completely eradicate these strong emotions, but rather that you *recognize* they're happening and where they came from.

....

Before we get into changing these emotions and the behaviors that result from them, I want to share a quick lesson on neuroplasticity. This is a fancy word for how the brain changes so that we can learn things like playing a new sport, speaking a new language, or making different and better financial decisions.

Our brains are amazing. Between each neuron are synapses. We have tons of these synapses as kids, but as adults, the amount is cut in half. That's because new experiences help us strengthen some of our connections, or neural pathways, and the others go away, known as synaptic pruning. This basically means that neural pathways get stronger the more we use them. This is how we adapt, and why it's easier to continue to think about things the way we've always thought about them.[1]

But we *can* change how we think. Now, no one does this overnight. If we did, we'd all be wealth-building masters who never react poorly to our partners suggesting that we move into a nicer home, one that mirrors our hard work and success but is a cost still within a healthy small percentage of our income. But I think you'll see that by noticing the thoughts that "just happened" and the strong emotions that "came out of nowhere," you'll gradually start thinking differently and acting differently, too.

Even reading this book is helping to change the way your brain fires around money. You're getting new information, and I'll be guiding you in making new decisions and taking small actions that help you rewire your entire mindset (and realities) around building wealth.

This should give you hope if you find yourself constantly in your own way. By noticing where your environments are creating strong thoughts that lead to strong emotions and in turn create poor decisions, you'll be able to think differently when it comes to your wealth.

THREE QUESTIONS TO SHIFT MONEY EMOTIONS

Take some time to write down your answers to these questions. Jot down anything that comes up! There's no right or wrong answer here. You're merely exploring where and when big emotions present themselves when it comes to your finances.

When do strong emotions show up around money? *Ex. Jealousy when someone buys a new house. Fear when you're checking your bank accounts. Anxiety when you hand over your credit card at a group dinner.* Check the QR code at the back of the book for more.

What money environment is at the heart of that emotion? *Ex. Scam Central, Money Desert, Torrential Rainy Day, Broke Millionaire, Ostriching, Pleasing and Helping.*

_____

_____

What is one small thing I could do differently in the future to minimize that emotion showing up? *Ex. Journal how you're feeling, do the thing you're avoiding, go for a walk, open this book to remind yourself which steps to take.*

_____

_____

You don't have to believe me, though. The proof is in so many stories of amazing people who haven't received a lick of financial advice but have changed their financial lives by understanding their money origins. Felicia is one of my favorite success stories. When we came together, she was in major credit card debt and pulling from her savings even while making a solid income. She had no idea how to build enough wealth to afford her first home, a longtime dream. I want to take you through Felicia's story, re-creating the questions I asked her so you can see how to take the same type of journey yourself.

Felicia's parents were the first in their families to go to college and the first to achieve a middle-class living. Her parents had stable jobs as a teacher and a plumber. With only one child to support, they were always hosting the extended family and providing big meals. If something broke in one of her uncle's houses, her dad was the first person they'd call either to come fix it or to pay the person who could. If any of the cousins ended up with a medical bill that their parents couldn't pay, Felicia's mom always offered money to ease the burden. Her parents often said that *helping is a fortune better than gold*. It was a mantra in their home. As a result, her family instilled the value of generosity, helping in any fashion they could, regardless of the financial impact.

However, there were times growing up when a family member or friend fell on particularly tough times. Felicia remembers her parents arguing about these situations any time they arose. There was an aunt who broke her leg and an uncle who totaled his car and needed a new one. Her dad would liquidate and sell everything they had if it was up to him. Felicia's mom often respectfully made the case that they had Felicia to think of—her college, her savings, her well-being. Otherwise they would "help themselves broke," her mother said. This would cause quite the reaction from her father, who felt bad for the good financial circumstances that their family was in compared to the instability of his siblings. It wasn't unfounded. Her cousins called her a "showboat" when she came to church with a new dress or new shoes. Thus there was often tension between Felicia's parents—how to help and by how much—which caused strife in the house. They wanted to live a good life and they wanted to be generous to their loved ones, but they didn't want to be "showboats." Their means made them self-conscious.

These experiences impacted Felicia. She learned that you could and should offset your success by being supergenerous with your friends and family members. If you're helping everyone who needs it, they won't resent you for making a bunch more money than them, or for getting a much higher-paying job or a bigger house.

Eventually this environment impacted Felicia's behaviors. From the time she started making meaningful money, she helped *everyone* in her family. She paid her cousin's medical bills. She paid for her parents' doctors. She paid her aunt's rent for an entire year. Her money went in each and every direction to help her relatives. Family was everything to her and she didn't see anything wrong with it. That is, until she started really looking at what she wanted for herself and how far away she was from those numbers.

At first Felicia had no idea that she was creating an obstacle to her dreams by helping everyone else out. Being generous with what she had was like breathing to her. But when we started looking at where her money went and what it was earning for her (we'll get to that in chapter 9), it was clear what was happening. Felicia was giving far too much of her income to other people to pay for their medical bills, rent, and school trips, and she was going into debt as a result. When we traveled back to her origin story, we suddenly understood. Felicia paid attention to every time she was asked for help and her initial inclination to say yes, to decide on the spot without thinking about it. She started noticing how often this was happening and how unconscious this behavior was. Once she became aware of her behavior and the mindset guiding it, she created a plan for deciding differently. I didn't ask her to stop helping, but rather to recognize her behavior so she could act in a way that would lead her to a healthier financial position.

The most important thing, which can seem like nothing at first, is acknowledging what's going on and becoming aware of what you're thinking and feeling in different situations. Remember not to blame yourself. It's not about fault. It comes from structural inequalities, your financial origins, and the money environments in which you were brought up.

You may not have inherited a bunch of cash, but I can promise that you inherited a belief system around money. We all did. Some of that is great, and some of that is not so great. You'll start paying attention to the "not so great" in the questions at the end of this chapter.

To begin building wealth we had to begin here—with understanding your mindset around money. Your mindset, or your relationship to wealth, is impacted by your financial origin stories. These are origins made up of your first experiences with money. The environment you grew up in—whether that was an environment of *Pleasing and Helping*, *Ostriching*, *Broke Millionaire*, *Torrential Rainy Day*, *Money Desert*, or *Scam Central*—created strong emotions around money that inform your decisions and can be detrimental to building wealth even if they don't seem like a bad thing on the surface (like me being frugal or Felicia trying to help everyone). Once you create an awareness of everything going on below the surface that influences your decisions, you can start making the right wealth-building decisions, one at a time, with my help throughout this book.

Examine your first experiences with money with these reflection prompts. Write down your answers in the space below:

What were your first experiences with money?

_____

_____

What environment(s) do you relate to the most?

_____

_____

What traits or behaviors did you notice in the people around you in these environments?

_____

_____

How are those experiences impacting your relationship with money today?

_____

_____

How is this showing up in your behaviors right now?

_____

_____

CHAPTER 3

Get Your Past Out of Your Future

TO GET YOUR PAST OUT OF YOUR FUTURE . . .

- Know the five most common financial pitfalls.
- Recognize where your financial education stopped.
- Overcome the naysayers and let them talk.

When I was clawing my way out of debt, I did *a lot* of journaling. Now, don't judge, but somehow I'd gone all these years helping people understand their financial origin stories without ever truly examining my own. When I first opened that turquoise leather journal, one I'd taken weeks to decide was the perfect place to begin excavating my limiting beliefs (because y'all know journaling doesn't work unless you have the perfect journal), I began to pour onto those pages all the things that haunted my subconscious about money. These beliefs kept me from raising my prices while I worked with clients, kept me quiet when I needed help, kept me working too much for too little, and caused me to question if I'd *really* become the megamillionaire I'd always dreamed of becoming.

As I look back at those journals today, I can see the beginnings of my rocket ship on those pages. By finally asking why—*why am I here, where am I, how did I arrive at this place, why is this happening to me*—I could acknowledge how my past was running major interference on my wealthy future. Those journal entries showed me where I was stuck in bad financial patterns and why. I saw how my desire to be perfect kept me from facing the not-so-perfect areas of my life and ostriching so as not to look at or deal with my failures and mishaps. There were also entries where indecision was paralyzing me. When you're facing financial ruin, you have to make decisions and make them fast, but I just couldn't.

Ultimately, I saw in those entries how hard it was to own the value I was bringing into other people's lives. Because I was a young, dark-skinned woman who was not from money, I believed I didn't deserve to charge what I was actually worth. But in that journal, I got back on track. I was able to let go of the mindsets creating pitfalls to my wealth-building journey. Pitfalls are our negative mindsets in action, creating hazards to financial success. But together we're going to be looking these pitfalls right in the eye—and combining them with your understanding from the last chapter about where they came from to put you in a solid place to disrupt them.

You're probably wondering how all this mindset stuff is showing up hard and fast in your day-to-day life. Y'all know I've worked with a *lot* of clients over the years—people with tons of money, people with no money, people with some money—and everybody has money behaviors holding them back (even me). When you're broke, you're letting these patterns run you. When you're wealthy, you've got control over these patterns even if they sometimes show up. Here are the pitfalls I see all the time. See if any of these resonate for you, because as we move through exciting decisions to make in these next chapters, we want to sidestep these pitfalls at every turn. You can't sidestep them if you don't see them, ya know?

As you go through the next sections, you'll see a few terms and their definitions:

MINDSETS: How you think about money, made up of your beliefs about money.

PITFALLS: hazards to your wealth-building journey. Your mindset in action.

TRIGGERS: situations that provoke you to make bad money decisions.

OBSTACLES: unforeseeable challenges to building wealth, big life events like losing a job or illness.

ISSUES: letting your mindset from your past rule your present and not having the awareness, knowledge, or courage to disrupt the mindset.

The Five Most Common Financial Pitfalls

1. Doing the Most

I see people who literally implement *everything*. All the financial advice they've ever heard. Whether it came from TikTok, MSNBC, or a book, they're trying it. They've got seven different retirement accounts, savings accounts, credit card accounts, and all sorts of accounts up the wazoo. Money is everywhere and nowhere because they keep opening accounts, moving it around, pulling it out, and shutting it down. They start businesses over here and invest some money over there. Their financial situation is getting worse because there's zero consistency, focus, or clear plan.

If *doing the most* sounds like you, think about why you go to a doctor. You go for a specific diagnosis, and you get a specific prescription for that diagnosis. This book is here to help you do the same. Through each chapter, you'll understand where your personal struggles are, and I'll give you tailored decisions to make to make progress. Making financial decisions specific to you *will* make a difference.

INSTEAD OF DOING THE MOST, pick one money problem you know you have and write it here:

_____

_____

Once you've gotten through the book and found the right solution, come back and write it here:

_____

_____

Focus on this solution until you're ready to focus on a new problem/ solution set.

_____

2. Overanalyzing

I see a lot of people who will analyze the terms on different retirement accounts or analyze stocks for months and refuse to make a choice. They are paralyzed. I get this. I have to keep this pitfall in check because it used to creep up on me. But when people do this, they miss out on so much more than if they just let it rock. Knowing the exact ins and outs of something before you make a move can result in lost opportunities. You also lose time, and time really matters for building wealth because every day you're not taking action to build wealth is a day your money is not compounding.

If *overanalyzing* is something you relate to, take a deep breath. I find it helpful to put a time cap on my decisions. As in: *Okay, Dominique, you have twenty-four hours to decide yes or no and then you're letting it go.* In that time, I'll make my list, understand the pros and cons, do the research I need, and then, one way or another, I'm moving along. That's my process, but yours might involve giving yourself a week or even a month to decide. Instead of pros and cons, you might make a decision tree, write out worst-case scenarios, read forums on the internet, or call one of your best friends. However, at some point you have to stop analyzing and start acting.

INSTEAD OF OVERANALYZING, write down one decision that you're overanalyzing here:

_____

_____

Now, circle the tool you'll use to decide:

PHONE A FRIEND   COST-BENEFIT ANALYSIS

PRO/CONS LIST   DECISION TREE   TIME CAP

WORST-CASE SCENARIO   RESEARCH 5 SOLUTIONS

When will you make your decision? ____/____/_____

3. Going for Instant Gratification

I've worked with people who want to fix fifteen years of financial ruin in twenty minutes. Or they want to become a millionaire by next Friday. But nothing meaningful ever happens instantly, as much as our social media lives want to say otherwise. These people let their impatience for wealth run their lives and views on money, instead of letting things take their natural time. You want to be patient in making the right decisions and do that consistently.

If *instant gratification* hits home for you (which it probably does for most of us), I promise to help you turn things around. Because you're choosing to go with me on this journey of wealth-building decisions, you'll see your fortunes shift sooner than you think. I'm often helped in moments of instant gratification by remembering the life of financial and time freedom I'm trying to design and asking myself if whatever I'm about to do is getting me closer to that or further away.

INSTEAD OF SEEKING INSTANT GRATIFICATION, ASK YOURSELF, is what I'm about to spend money on going to get me closer to my dream life or further away?

If it's not bringing you closer to wealth, slow down and let the impulse pass by imagining your dream life.

4. Starting, but Not Finishing

Starters/not finishers are the same people who never finish taking the antibiotic and wonder why they don't get better. You gotta finish the dang pack and not just stop when the symptoms chill. Similarly, these individuals often start making changes with a lot of passion, sprinting out of the gate. They look for ways to grow their money and maybe they're even doing a great job of saving. But then they'll pour every dollar they have on something that doesn't make sense—like a huge, international trip or a fancy new bag that they just decided to click and pay for. These people don't seem to realize that there's a right way and a wrong way to spend your money. Putting away money just to go splurge and be back at ground zero (or below) with no money to cover your ass and no money growing leads to a vicious cycle of starting and not finishing.

If you're a starter/not finisher, you need to practice sticking with the path and decisions that are actually going to help you. Look at all the big purchases you made in the last year or two and determine if they helped your money grow or if they just wasted money. Realizing how often you splurge and where you're setting yourself back will give you pause the next time you do it.

INSTEAD OF STARTING BUT NOT FINISHING, list three big purchases you made in the last two years:

1.

2.

3.

Did they help your money grow or waste it?

_____

_____

_____

If you were to go back in time, would you spend money in the same way?

_____

_____

_____

5. Avoiding Risk

When people avoid risk, they avoid wealth. I get it. Risk is scary and understanding a risk often means understanding a new idea. But all wealth-building involves some risk. Starting a business is a risk.

Investing your money is a risk. Investing your time in figuring this out with me is a risk (which will pay off majorly). Investing in the stock market is a risk. But to build wealth, you have to do things outside of just saving, outside of just working.

If you're someone who's *avoiding risk*, I'm about to lay down some knowledge in these next chapters that's going to make you feel more secure. You've already started the journey by opening up this book, which is more than most people will do. As we go through this wealth-building journey together, I want you to notice where you're scared to start or where you're avoiding the decisions I'm asking you to make. Take action anyway, even if it's something small that feels more comfortable.

INSTEAD OF AVOIDING RISK, ASK, what mini-risk can I take this week that puts me outside of my comfort zone?

_____

_____

_____

For example: Finishing this book and implementing one step into my life! Having that money conversation from the last chapter!

At the core of all these financial pitfalls is the same thing. You're letting your past run your future. Most of these pitfalls are brought on by triggers (like hanging out with your girlfriends who love to shop), psychological issues (like letting your money origin stories from the past rule your present day), or obstacles (big life events that you can't control, such as injury, illness, or job loss).

Now that you realize what your negative money patterns are and where they came from, try to leave your past challenges behind. If every time you're with your girls and you're complaining about the past—what happened to you, why you're broke, how you can't pay for anything, how the bills are piling up—consider that it's not helping. I know it can feel good to let off a little bit of steam and frustration for what you're going through, but it truly doesn't work because it doesn't change anything.

Actually, it makes you feel worse. There's plenty of literature[1] out there that says venting doesn't help make the person feel better unless it's done with someone who can help you deconstruct the situation and create meaning out of what happened. Take people on rant sites. Two studies published in "Anger on the Internet: The Perceived Value of Rant-Sites" found that the mood of visitors, both those reading and writing, is worse after.[2] Not better. So, if you're going to vent, do it wisely. Pick one friend who won't add fuel to your fire but rather will help you decide how best to move forward and talk to them. Just don't go around to everyone you know bitching about being broke.

Instead of spending time and energy complaining, spend it understanding, paying attention, and making different decisions from here on out. I'm not saying don't talk about your money, because obviously I told you earlier to have conversations about it to regain control. I'm just saying don't add firewood to an open flame and expect it to go out. It won't. Venting is firewood.

Where Your Education Stopped

When I was growing up, I was told to save my money, but I wasn't told what else to do. Sure, I knew the importance of paying bills, looking at numbers, and having some reserves, but that's pretty much where it ended for me. Luckily, I had an interest in money so I got not one but two degrees that helped me understand how to build wealth. And I still managed to go broke, y'all. But that's because I missed a lot of the basics. I missed a lot of the reflection we've already done together. When I think about financial education, I see a very specific journey:

WEALTH EDUCATION
Basic: Saving and spending
Intermediate: Debt
Advanced: Investing

First, we have to make up for the education we didn't get, and then we need to talk to kids about money so we can build generational wealth.

Basic: When you're a kid, you don't have any personal bills, right? Whether you get money from walking a dog or an allowance or a birthday card using your daddy's food stamps on Häagen-Dazs (guilty), you don't have a ton of financial responsibility even if things aren't going well for your family. Then you make those first financial decisions, whether you were educated to do so or not. Maybe that's in high school, or maybe it's earlier or later. Whether you bought your own first car, took a date to homecoming and bought the suit or dress or flower for that, or you paid for your college application fees, you saved up to spend your money on something that mattered for you.

You were literally creating your first financial strategy. Money came in, you saved it, and you decided what you wanted to spend it on.

But then you either went to college or to live and work on your own. Regardless of the exact time line, eventually everyone's next step involved a job, and then you had bills to pay. You might have paid rent for the first time, signing documents that made you financially responsible and liable.

Intermediate: The moment you took out your first debt, you entered a new system. Whether you racked up money on a credit card, took out a college loan that you had to repay, or got your first mortgage, *boom*, you were instantly exposed to the American way. When people don't understand how debt works—which is most—it can cripple them. Every month, they're either racking up interest or sending all their money to their college loans, so they take out more credit. This is where people's education either stops or significantly slows down. It's where I see most people hitting a brick wall because financially, they can't do more than pay their debt and eat. They try to save something, but it's not moving the needle toward wealth. It's where they end.

Advanced: Most people never make it to the stage of getting past debt and building wealth. They don't know the strategies that allow money to make money, like how to get into markets, what to do in real estate, and where to invest. People who have this education know that wealth does not just fall into your lap. It happens very intentionally. That's why they're cool to grab the six-dollar cup of coffee. They figure they should drink their expensive coffee if it brings them joy, because the goal is so much bigger than those six dollars. These people know that taking their wealth to the next level requires other people, requires consistency, requires risk. And it's so much more than saving and spending, which was where my own journey initially stopped.

DO YOU KNOW WHERE YOUR FINANCIAL EDUCATION STOPPED?

Circle: *Basic, Intermediate, Advanced*

No matter your answer, don't fret. Instead get excited, because I'm about to complete that wealth education for you one decision at a time throughout this book. As you journey to more advanced education, you're going to know more, which means you're going to *build* more.

Your financial literacy will result in making more money and achieving new wealth goals for yourself, but the people around you might not understand because they don't have the financial education themselves. It's my experience that when people don't know something, they're quick to cut it down or dismiss it. You might feel the effects of that as your wealth grows. While I hope that you take what you're learning and share it with others, I also hope that you don't believe what the haters say about you, because it's a projection of their own limited money beliefs.

Overcome the Naysayers and Let Them Talk

Forbes published a profile on me titled "How a Financial Planner Went from Broke to Generating $8.5 Million" and I couldn't read it. For weeks. I had tossed and turned about whether to let someone write about my experience and my numbers. When I first got the interview request, I called my chief of staff, saying: "Yo, what do you think about this? Should I let them write it?" She told me I should. She said it would empower more women, more women of color, and more moms that they could build back from broke. I prayed about the decision to do the interview and asked my then-partner and friends their opinions, but everyone told me the same thing: people like me exist to serve.

But I was terrified. I was scared of what people were going to say. I was scared they would call me a fraud. I was scared my community would look at me differently. I was scared people would start asking me for money. I was scared my family and friends would start treating me differently. Because it can happen, right?

Ultimately, I read it and was so happy with how the writer, Geri, captured my story. To see a narrative that once caused me so much pain, stress, and embarrassment framed in a way that empowered others, well, it's hard to describe how good that felt!

My fear represents the underbelly no one talks about when we start dreaming for more and believing we can get it. Aiming for a life of wealth can feel lofty and very wild sometimes. There are fears of what it will take to get there, fears of what happens if you get it and lose it, and fears of what people will say about your desire for a bigger life. I had stated what I believed was possible for myself—being a millionaire, starting a financial company to help people, becoming a digital nomad for a year, traveling the world with children—and people have flat out told me that it's crazy. How could you possibly do that? Well, this type of response just means you're sharing your financial goals with the wrong person. If you can create a vision for your financial future that you're writing down and saying out loud—then that's just who you are and it's what you've decided you deserve. Nobody's opinion can take that away from you. You've got to stay close to your center of gravity as people try to knock you off. Because they will.

When I was building my business, I had so many people tell me to get a "real" job. Writing my own paycheck *is* a real job, and my paycheck means as much as one that comes from someone else. People telling me to get a "real" job just wanted to protect me, and I get it. So I went to those interviews. I considered it, but all I kept thinking when I was considering the positions and talking to the hiring managers was *this is going to kill my dreams.*

Here's another thing. Many people simply aren't qualified to advise you because they've never built wealth. They've never taken a risk or been in your shoes. I want you always to think about your source. Who are you hearing this from? What are their experiences? If you can understand where their point of view is coming from, you can better understand what to do with what they say. Ultimately you have to decide your own path forward, and it won't always be easy or carefree.

Even the people closest to you may knock you down as you're on your way up. Recently I reminded myself that I've always dreamed of being wealthy. When I was in high school, I wrote over and over again in my notebooks: *Miss Future Millionaire*. I told myself from early on that this was where I was gonna be, that this was what I was going to manifest. When you know in your heart of hearts what wealth you dream for yourself, nobody can rob you of where you're projected to go.

My dad was planning to buy a new place to live and has an old 1985 Mercedes SL 300 that I used as a kid. I practically drove it to the ground in high school and I always said I wanted to restore it one day when I made some money. Well, he was planning on giving the car away before he moved into the new house, and I had an idea to help him with both! I said, "Listen, I'll buy the car from you so I can make my dream come true and restore it for myself, which will be *expensive* but worth it for my nostalgia." I thought this was a great situation. My dad would make money on something he was just planning to give away. While I was at it, I said, "If you're open to it, tell me what home you're looking to buy and maybe I'll purchase it and rent it back to you. That way you can have something a little nicer and I can expand my investments." Instead of being enthusiastic, though, my dad seemed down.

Well, he kept looking at houses without sharing any information with me. Not even a Zillow link. Finally, I wanted to know what was going on. Eventually he suggested I give him the money I was spending on his car and he'd use that to buy his house. As I mentioned earlier, my dad was supercheap when I was growing up, once he was out of jail. Now I was brought back to my childhood days when he never wanted to help my mom and me with money. He accused me of being better than everyone. He said I was always this way, spending his food stamps on unreasonable things when I was a kid. He just let those criticisms fly.

Honestly, y'all, I was cracking up. Because I know who I am. I know I'm generous. I know I've always liked what I've liked. Of course his comments bothered me, but not enough to make bad decisions just to please my father. But as you start claiming your future and designing a life that's worthy and wealthy, you can't let what people think and say tempt you to change course. If you let people's ideas determine what you pursue, you'll delay your journey to wealth. I know because I let personal and societal sources of criticism control me for a long time. Eventually you realize that the only one who benefits from doing what other people want is them. Sometimes the naysayers aren't saying anything exactly; it's their actions that show how little they believe in you.

During the years I was cobbling my way back to financial stability, I went after a financial literacy contract with the federal government. So, I met with this guy and delivered my presentation. Then we met a second time. At the end, instead of offering me a contract, he offered me a monthly retainer and condo downtown to be his girlfriend, y'all. He was a married man with kids and a prestigious job! I gave him a flat no and never submitted my proposal. This man did not believe in my worth or my expertise as a serious professional. I was so thrown off, I stopped pursuing my then-goal of landing a big government contract. He killed that dream for me and threatened my confidence.

When you're out in the world following your own internal compass, you'll bump up against things that threaten to keep you small, disappoint you, and cause you to second-guess. To create things you've never had is a risk, and risk means there's a potential for pain, sweat, and tears. Instead of focusing on what people are saying or implying about you, stay focused on preparing for that bigger step in your life, like getting a dog, going on a vacation, or investing in your professional development—whatever those bigger dreams are for you that will be made possible by wealth. It's probably going to mean that you're uncomfortable.

For example, right now I'm preparing for the day I have a billion-dollar company, even though there are a lot of people who don't believe I will get there. It's big. I say it out loud at least once a day just so I can hear it louder than I hear the critics and make sure I subconsciously believe it as well. I'm not making moves to make as much as I did last year. I am making moves for a billion. That's what I'm preparing for, and what I have to remind myself of when I'm doing uncomfortable things like hiring more people, handing over financial control to a CFO, and letting myself be profiled in the media. Don't let people's doubts keep you from preparing. Whatever expansion you're shying away from for fear of people talking, or whatever decisions make you uncomfortable as you work through this book—whether that's acknowledging your debt-free dreams or making your first investment—I want you to ask what I ask myself: *Am I delaying my success because I'm scared of what people will say?*

It's okay if you answer yes, but find a small way to keep moving anyway.

QUESTIONS TO KEEP YOURSELF ACCOUNTABLE
FOR YOUR SPENDING

Get out a pen and jot down your answers to the following questions:

What dollar amount do you consider a large transaction for yourself (not including rent, mortgage, utilities, etc.)?

_____

_____

Write down the last five times you spent this much money and what you spent it on.

_____

_____

Rewrite the ones that you would *not* do over again . . .

_____

_____

Were you triggered by anything going on in your own life and anyone with or around you at the time that might have led to this purchase?

_____

_____

Were you displaying any unhelpful mindsets about your wealth that played into these purchases?

_____

_____

Were you facing any real-life obstacles that caused this purchase?

_____

_____

Reflect on these answers to examine where your money goes and why. Money is rarely nonemotional when you're struggling with it.

CHAPTER 4

Be the CEO of Your Money

TO BE THE CEO OF YOUR MONEY YOU WILL . . .

- Create your vision through lifestyle design.
- Assemble your personal wealth advisory board.
- Reinforce positive beliefs with new money mantras.

As chief executive officer of my own company, I make decisions throughout the day that keep my business functioning, profitable, and a brand people love—including my employees! The train stays on track because of me. Being the CEO affects how I think, and how I move throughout my day and throughout my life. It's the lens through which I see everything, how I understand that I'm in charge and that no one is coming to fix things for me. I can't be the victim of circumstance because my entire team will suffer. I'm constantly solution oriented. If we have a technology glitch, if we have a team member who quits, or if we have an opportunity we're unsure about, I'm always going to figure it out. It's as simple as that. You can throw whatever you want my way. The average person might shut down, but I thrive because I have to. I'm always thinking about growing my company and making my company work not only for my team and for me, but also for our community. That focus starts the moment I wake up.

Even if you're not a CEO, you can be the CEO of your wealth. The company you're presiding over is your money, or the sum of your personal finances. When you see yourself this way, it fundamentally shifts how you look at, think about, and handle your money. You're in charge. You deserve to be in charge, because you've just spent the last two chapters understanding what formed your thinking and thus your habits around money.

Now it's time to step up and become the CEO of your soon-to-be wealthy life. A CEO has four important qualities:

1. They oversee everything that happens at their company.
2. They have a vision for where the company is going.
3. They have an advisory board of people to turn to.
4. They keep their thoughts in check and in control, even when it's hard.

You'll be applying these same qualities to your finances since you're the CEO of your money.

It's okay if you've never been the CEO of a business or taken command of your finances before. I'm going to walk you through what it looks and feels like so you can begin moving differently tomorrow, moving like you're in charge.

Being in charge starts from the moment your day begins. Most people open their eyes and check social media. Well, I wake up and look at my accounts. I literally look at every single bank account in the morning, every single credit card, because I'm the person in charge. It's very similar to checking in with my team—*How are you? Did anything happen overnight? Where can I support you today?* It starts with being aware. I have dashboards for our business so at any point during the day, I can see exactly how key metrics are growing. I review the increase in our monthly recurring revenue, the growth of our email list and social media accounts, conversion rates and daily sales of all our products, as well as our expenses.

This is akin to having a snapshot of your personal finances at any moment—like income into checking accounts, retirement brokerage accounts, real estate holdings, spending, and debts. You've got to know what's going on. If you don't, nobody will. Your money is your business. Checking in with your dollars is like checking in with your team and making sure they're in a position to succeed. If you're not looking every day and you're letting your money come and go however it pleases, that's like having an unruly staff that doesn't do its job. Your business won't get very far if the people who work for you aren't showing up.

Then, as you jump into your day, things are going to come your way, and they'll come your way fast. Because you're in charge now, you don't get to complain and hope someone else deals with it. *You* are the someone else. This shows up in simple things like getting up, getting in the car, and driving to work in traffic. You don't let that ruin your day. You don't sink because nothing is going your way. Instead you turn it around. You make those twenty extra minutes in the car work for you. You turn on a podcast that expands your thinking around how to generate wealth. Maybe you decide to learn about real estate investing. You choose how getting stuck in traffic affects you. You can get pissed off and angry for twenty minutes and waste time, or you can change your mindset. People who are in charge of their finances take every opportunity to see the glass half-full and find a solution that will grow the business that is their life.

Throughout their average day, a CEO is constantly thinking about opportunities for growth. Not only as an individual leader, but also as a company. So you, as the leader of your money, should be looking everywhere for moneymaking opportunities, whether it's something you want to execute now or something you want to look into in the future—like an opportunity to make extra money dog-sitting to pay down your credit card bill this month or an opportunity to sell an old record that's going viral on TikTok. Additionally, CEOs are always looking for ways to save money, so if you see that you're not using that recurring subscription, even if it's just four dollars, get rid of it. Or, if your home internet service comes with a hefty price tag, call around and see if you can get a better price.

CEOs are responsible for guiding their organizations in a big-picture vision. You stay in charge when you have something grander in mind that you're working toward, perhaps having more time in your day by outsourcing chores or engaging in more creative pursuits like songwriting. As the CEO of your money, having this type of vision for your life is mandatory. Knowing what's important to you beyond just getting rich is something the best CEOs have in common. They have a purpose that drives them to think bigger and keep moving forward, and they've figured that out by imagining their ideal life.

Lifestyle Design

The process of lifestyle design requires asking yourself what you want your life to look and feel like. This book is inherently about creating that beautiful, wealthy life you've dared to dream about and are now taking steps to actually live. But you've gotta know what that life looks like for you. Building wealth means very different things to different people. We don't want to put an exact number on it. We want to put a feeling on it. Sometimes we get so mired in the thick of surviving, of crawling out of debt, of overthinking our investment strategies, that we forget to ask ourselves why . . . Why am I even doing this?

When you decide to build wealth, you're deciding so much more than things you want to buy. You're establishing a vision for your life, too. You're deciding what you want your life to feel like and where you want to go. When it comes to your finances, you don't just want to know which assets you want to buy, or how much you want in your savings; you want a purpose for building wealth to begin with.

Remember at the beginning of the book, when I mentioned how wealth means different things to different people? How for some people it means creating millions of dollars, while for others it means traveling the world with a single backpack? I'd like you to take the opportunity now to consider your own definition of wealth. You might build financial wealth to afford the best health care and stay healthy, or to buy a home that allows you to be near your family. Like we've talked about, no two people define wealth the same . . . and that's okay. What matters most is that you can say, "I know what wealth means for me."

To take the next step toward creating your plan for that wealth, it's important to have a very specific picture for what your wealthy life looks like. For example, have you ever taken the time to think about the last day of your life? Let's say, hopefully, that I die a peaceful death in my sleep at 110 years old. Where am I? Am I by myself? Am I surrounded by children and grandchildren? Do I have friends there by my side? Or maybe an ol' wrinkly husband? And where is this all happening? Am I in a condo or a house? I literally ask myself these questions sometimes.

Before we get into designing the picture that your wealth will enable, I want to know why you want to build wealth. This is your intention. It's the engine that powers your decisions. It's bigger than cars, clothes, houses, and dollar amounts. It's reasoning. It's passion. It's *why*. When you're not feeling motivated to create change, it's because you don't have your why, or you haven't been intentionally connecting to it.

When I ask community members who participate in my wealth-building master classes why they've joined, I hear things like the following:

To support my family.

To learn how to make my money work for me.

To have a better understanding of how money works.

To be able to retire.

To have wealth that can be passed down to the next generation.

To create another stream of income.

Let's start with *your* big why. Think about why you paid the money for this book. I know it's not just because it had a great cover. Your honest answer will be what helps you finish reading and implement my strategies. It will carry you through when days are hard or you're not feeling it.

Now, jot down . . . **Why** are you building wealth?

_____

_____

_____

_____

_____

_____

_____

My "why" for building wealth is threefold, a detail I often share with my students. First, I'm doing what I do to create an amazing life for myself, my daughters, and my other family. My wealthy life is low-stress, in which financial freedom allows me to get help for the things I hate doing (such as cleaning and cooking). I can go where I want, how I want, and have the best care and education for my daughters wherever we are. If I want to get the girls on a plane to Costa Rica and live there for a year, I can do that and have the money to hire child care, tutors, and a villa without worrying about paying for the mortgage on an empty house. It means we have the freedom to constantly experience new things, whether that's travel, hobbies, or a collection of cars. Second, I love educating others and providing information, and I want to do this work for as long as I can be helpful. And last, I'm creating generational wealth and a legacy so that one day, my great-grandkids can talk about how Grandma B left them with financial security and the lessons to grow it for generations to come. Those are *my* reasons. Knowing your why is your mission statement for lifestyle design.

Let's get to designing your wealthy lifestyle . . .

This process is always exhilarating because it's here that you start to envision what "feeling rich" is all about. I'm now going to take you through some prompts that walk you through a day in your ideal life.

Imagine you wake up wealthy. What does it feel like not to have any debt, to have financial freedom, to have everything you need? What's it going to feel like when you can support anyone who needs support, buy things you desire, and check your investments to see that you're way up?

Where are you when you're waking up? What does your place look like? Who are you surrounded by? What does it smell like? What are you drinking and eating for breakfast? What kind of clothes are you getting dressed in? Look in the mirror and see your wealthy self. What do you look like?

When you think about this wealthy day, picture all the details. Think about your work. Your social life. Where you spend your money and your time. Walk yourself through it and envision it all, channeling wealth and abundance every step of the way. Let that guide how you feel and what you see.

If you'd prefer to close your eyes and listen to me guide you through these prompts, you can find an audio recording at the QR code in the back of the book.

When I've done this exercise in the past, it helped create the life I'm living now. I saw water glistening behind me. I envisioned drinking the freshest orange juice with loved ones by my side. Now I literally do that each morning thanks to our family chef. Then I go over to my computer in my office on the fortieth floor, with the Intracoastal Waterway sparkling behind me. I chose this way of life before I ever lived it.

One of my students designed her life, and she designed a life in which, at every moment, she felt, *I can breathe.* That was powerful for me, because I remembered back to the days when I was in terrible debt. I also felt like I *couldn't* breathe. I have asthma, so it was literal. I want the life that you're envisioning to provide a huge breath of fresh air. Maybe you're designing a day when your bills are on autopay because there's always enough to withdraw. Maybe your designed day has iced coffee delivered while you're building your business. These moments might seem small, but they carry huge energy and insights.

Now, once you can see the vision for your lifestyle and have designed your dream down to the details of your day, you can get granular and decide exactly what you need to do to make this dream a reality.

For example, in my recent lifestyle design, I envisioned a real estate portfolio, but at the time, I didn't own any homes. I asked myself, if I wanted a real estate portfolio to create passive income and then serve as wealth to be passed on to my children, what must I do about that today? Well, I must purchase some houses, and how must I purchase houses? I must get preapproval, get an agent, do market research, etc. In other words, I took a larger lifestyle vision and broke it down into smaller steps. Now you give it a try, starting with one financial goal you'd like to make possible in the near future, such as buying your first house or saving $20,000 toward a new business. Write down your answer to the following questions:

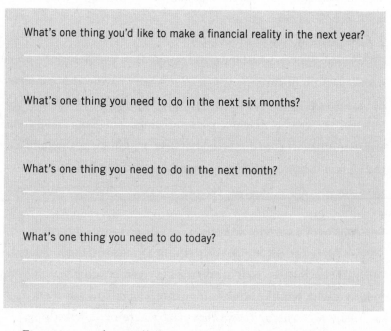

What's one thing you'd like to make a financial reality in the next year?

What's one thing you need to do in the next six months?

What's one thing you need to do in the next month?

What's one thing you need to do today?

Figuring out the small things is important because if you create wealth just to cross a goal off like buying a house, what happens after that? If you don't know *why*, it's really easy to screw up your finances because you have no vision past attaining something. This activity will be something you can always come back to but it will serve as important motivation. When you're the CEO of your life and your money in every moment—big and small—before you know it, the lifestyle you're designing in these pages will become a reality.

Your Wealth-Building Advisory Board

Just as CEOs have an advisory board they consult about business decisions, millionaires who are the CEOs of their money have wealth-building advisory boards, too. If you pay attention to wealthy people, you'll notice they have something in common: their conversations about money just hit differently. First of all, they're willing to have them. Second, they know who to have them with: people who are open-minded, generous, supportive, and on a wealth-building journey themselves.

Wealthy conversations leave you feeling full. You don't have to be surrounded by financially rich people to start having rich conversations. Instead, just try them with the people you'll identify below. To build an advisory board with which you can have ongoing money conversations (like what to do about your debt, which savings account has the highest interest rate, how to negotiate your next job offer, how to apply for your first mortgage, etc.), I want you to consider four people:

Someone with a wealthy mindset—this person is always there to pump you up, encourage you to think abundantly about money, and help you keep your eye on the life you're creating.

Someone with wealthy ideas—this person can talk to you about books, podcasts, and posts that make you think differently about money.

Someone with wealthy information—this person is always consuming information, meeting people, and introducing you to resources and connections that help you on your wealth-building journey.

Someone with wealthy strategies—this person assists you in choosing a financial direction.

Together these individuals comprise your wealth-building advisory board. Communicate with them regularly, as they are your allies and supporters as you continue down your path of wealth. These are the few people who won't look at you like you're crazy when you say you want to be a millionaire or have wealth that you can transfer to your kids! As you step into your role as the CEO of your finances, these dialogue starters may help while talking to your wealth-building advisory board members:

What book expanded your point of view lately?
What's the best piece of advice you were given in the last month?
What does wealth mean to you?
What's one thing you do each day that leaves you feeling fulfilled?

Whenever I'm spending time with one particular group of good friends (mostly people of color), who are both my peers and millionaires themselves, we talk about the challenges, successes, and money moves we're making. They're my advisory board. The conversations I have with them are fundamentally different from conversations I have with anyone else. We share the books that have been most influential on our abundance mindset. We exchange strategies for investments and taxes. We talk about how it feels to embody our worth as our wealth scales. We openly air lessons and missteps so we can learn from each other. Each person is honest, helpful, and noncompetitive, always championing the group's collective success. Conversations like these expand my vision for what's possible.

Look, every conversation you have with your friends doesn't have to be about money. I'll talk about celebrity gossip with the best of them. For these discussions to grow and challenge us, it's actually better if you have them with specific people you've identified who are on their own wealth-building journeys.

Consider one of my community members, Minda. Minda started having conversations like these with a friend, Leena, whom she eventually chose for her wealth-building advisory board. Over dinner, Minda shared a negotiation podcast with Leena, who she thought would appreciate it because she worked in sales and was a skilled negotiator. A month later, when Minda was recruited for a new job, she asked Leena's advice while negotiating the offer. In that conversation, Leena and Minda role-played her negotiation, and Minda was able to secure 70 percent more than what she was currently making.

In these conversations, we exchange seeds of ideas and information that will bloom later, just like they did for Minda.

Make sure that you're having regular conversations about your financial journey with your wealth-building advisory board. Through these conversations, you'll get the motivation, ideas, and strategies you need to do the hard and consistent work of being the CEO of your money.

Develop Your Money Mantras

There are only a few things that I do the same way, without fail, every day. I check my numbers. I pray. And I say my money mantras—short, positive declarations that elevate my energy and my mindset no matter what's happening that day.

When I was broke, I prayed every time I logged in to my bank accounts that there would be a positive balance. I needed enough money there to pay my bills. During that time, I knew God would have my back, but over time, I realized that I needed to have my own. I needed to do more than hope and pray when I looked at my finances. God gave me strength, but what I did with that strength was up to me. So I decided my actions should reflect the fact that I was the CEO of my money and my life. I created mantras to repeat every time I checked my accounts. Instead of desperately praying, I positively announced the mantra: *I'm in control of my wealth.*

Mantras are meant to change your thinking, which will in turn change what you're feeling, which will in turn change your actions. Being the CEO of your money will not always be easy, but your mantras will keep you feeling in control even when times are hard.

Take one of my students, Gabriella. She used to think to herself, *I'm so bad with money.* Every time she did this, she felt really down on herself. When she felt down on herself, she would shop online to feel better, which would cause her to spend more money than she had, which would make her think, *I'm so bad with money.* The destructive cycle would continue.

When Gabriella shifted the voice in her head to a mantra that said, *I'm great with money,* she felt more in control of her finances. She trusted herself to make good decisions. When she had a bad day and wanted to shop, she'd repeat, *I'm great with money,* and exit out of her shopping cart before she completed the purchase.

This is how these short sentences can work. They shift what you're thinking so that you focus on better thoughts, then feel better, then act better. Mantras keep your mind focused on what's possible with money, not on what's wrong.

The CEO of one's finances doesn't log in to their bank accounts thinking, *I hope there's enough.* They think, *I have everything I need.*

They don't invest their money and think, *This will never work.* They think, *Wealth always flows back to me.*

They don't apply for a loan and think, *I'll never be approved.* They think, *My opportunities are limitless.*

Mantras remind you that you're in control of your money and that you're destined to build wealth by programming your thinking with positive thoughts. When I look back to the time I was writing "Miss Future Millionaire" over and over again in high school, I realize I've been using money mantras all along. Now, however, I'm much more specific and thoughtful about what I'm saying to myself and when.

Let's take a look at the money mantras I use every day so that you can start thinking about yours . . .

I'm a money magnet.
Money flows to me easily.
I've made the decision to become wealthy.
There's always more than enough money in my life.
My income is constantly increasing.
I am wealthy in more than one way.

These mantras work because they evoke strong and worthy feelings around money (for me). Money flows to me naturally and I do not have to worry, fret, or panic about it. There have been times in my life where I've blocked money and sabotaged it coming my way due to my old and limiting beliefs. By letting go of those old money stories, I'm always attracting new opportunities.

Once I've decided something, my intention is in motion to make my desired outcome happen. Now I just need to make the choices to see the fruits of that decision, just as you will see the fruits of yours throughout this book.

Everyone has different mantras that resonate with them. There is no right or wrong way to have a mantra. You simply want to declare something that rings true about your relationship with money, where you might need some strength, and use that as a starting point.

Here are some examples to consider from students in my Finances Demystified community:

I attract abundance.
I love and appreciate everything I have.
Wealth is on its way.
I am magnetic to money.
Money loves me.

Try writing out a few different versions or picking from ones you see here. If, when you read and say one of these mantras, you feel an infusion of strength or positivity, you'll know you've hit the jackpot. That's your money mantra. Use it.

The way that you use these mantras in your daily life is unique to you. Maybe you write them on your mirror or put them as recurring calendar invites in your phone. Maybe you say them every time you look at your bank accounts. What matters is that you're working them so they can work for you. They will help you stay in command as the talented CEO of your money that you are.

CHAPTER 5

Know Your Numbers

COUNT TO FIVE TO KNOW YOUR NUMBERS

- Look at your finances every day.
- Calculate your two magic numbers and your bottom line.
- Take steps to turn your bottom-line number positive if it isn't already.
- Determine your net worth.
- Create milestones to increase your net worth.

know if someone is on a secure path to wealth by their answer to a single question: *Do you know how much you make each month?* It tells me everything I need to know. It tells me if they're looking at their numbers and whether or not they have a financial plan. You simply cannot have a wealth-building plan if you do not know what money you're making decisions with.

When I was going through my financial hardship, I absolutely could not answer this question, evidenced by the fact I paid $40 for a single cup of coffee, not once but many times. Let me tell you, it wasn't because that coffee was dope and dripping in gold. It was because I was oblivious to what was going on. I thought that thing was costing me five bucks, but I was very wrong. At a time I couldn't afford to be wrong.

My $5 coffee became $40 every time I paid with my debit card. How is that possible, you might be wondering? There's no such thing as a $40 cup of joe. Well, if you're not paying attention, yeah, a cup of coffee can be $40. You see, I had not looked at my bank account for weeks and weeks. I ignored my finances because I didn't want to accept or address what I had a hunch was the reality: things were not good. With nothing more than a rough estimate in my brain of what might be in there, I kept spending whatever money I thought I had. Often, my estimates were off.

Then, one day, my debit card was declined when I was trying to get gas. I finally looked at my account and noticed I was in the negative by some $900, of which $600 was from checking account overdraft fees. Every time I'd withdrawn from my account in the previous weeks, whether it was for my $5 coffee, $10 Netflix subscription, or $100 grocery run, I was charged $35 *per transaction* as an overdraft fee. Thirty-five dollar overdraft transaction fee + $5 coffee = $40 coffee. This meant that the few times I'd gotten my favorite coffee, it was eight times the price on the register. I love coffee, but not for $40, and definitely not when I'm broke. It made my stomach turn.

I immediately called the bank and told them to remove the overdraft protection function on my account. Back when I had money, if the account overdrafted, it would be pulled from my savings. But I didn't have any savings left, so if overdraft protection stayed on, it meant I owed the bank money that I couldn't pay back.

I never would have been in this situation if I had been looking at my numbers with any regularity. I would have known what the hell was going on. When I started the very simple activity of looking at my numbers every day, everything shifted. At first, this meant that I was reviewing just transactions in my one checking account and my debts from unpaid bills and collection agencies. But I felt a sense of control knowing exactly what opportunities and challenges I had on my hands. I had all the numbers down in this old-school spreadsheet that I would track every day. As time went on, I not only looked at what was coming in and what I owed, but I also started reviewing my growing savings account and investments, which was energizing and pushed me to keep progressing.

Today I have a rich portfolio of multiple checking accounts, credit cards, retirement accounts, money in the stock market, and real estate. I get excited when I look at it, which I still do every day. Sometimes more than once. Even now that I'm wealthy, this practice is important to me because it keeps me in control of my finances and operating as the CEO like we talked about before!

You can't make money moves if you don't know what's going on.
You really can't.

I know when things are bad, or meh, or just not where you want them to be, it's easy to avoid looking at them. Maybe you're scared or maybe you simply haven't had time. Well, you made time for this book and this book won't work for you unless you're willing to dive in. Realize that having data means you can create solutions. You'll be in a position to figure out what needs to be adjusted or shifted. You'll be motivated to keep making the decisions that will positively impact your wealth. You'll be aware instead of in the dark.

In the past, when my clients and students haven't wanted to look at their numbers, it's been because they feel like whatever is on paper won't match up with the visions they have of themselves or their plans and goals for their lives. They worry that the numbers will tell them they aren't where they are supposed to be by this age or stage of life. But while looking at your numbers is like looking in a mirror, it's also like turning the lights on. It gives you information that makes building wealth infinitely easier.

Many times, people don't look at their numbers until it's too late. When they finally do, they've either paid $40 for a coffee and owe a grand more, or they have an unbelievable opportunity to rent or buy an amazing spot and aren't in the financial position to say yes. People often don't pull their numbers together until there is a major life event that forces the issue, and by that time they've lost out on time and opportunities.

Knowing your numbers is easier than you think it is and doesn't take as much time, either. It starts with the simple act of logging in to your bank accounts.

Two Magic Numbers

The majority of my clients and students cannot tell me exactly how much money is hitting their bank accounts each month after taxes. So, you start here, the first of the two magic numbers. This is the amount you'll be able to put toward debt, expenses, savings, and investments. This is the number that we'll be putting to work in future chapters.

The second of the two magic numbers is your expenses. This is everything that you spend money on in a month. When every dollar is accounted for, we'll subtract your expenses from your income and see what we get.

Magic Number #1: What money is coming in every month.
Magic Number #2: What money is being spent every month.

Let's break down this exercise. Let's talk more about the first magic number, **your income** . . .

The first magic number, your income, includes any money that you have from a full-time job, a part-time job, rental income, gigs, etc. Count it all.

I know many of you are hustling and either your monthly base income might vary or your side-hustle money might change every month. But everyone has an average, and everyone has a bare minimum amount they're bringing in. If your income is always changing, focus on finding your average monthly income over the last six months or year. Let's say you're a real estate agent and there are some months you bring in as little as $2,000 and some months you bring in as much as $15,000, but your average is about $6,000 a month. With this average number, you'll be in a better position to plan and budget during the low months without blowing it during the high months. So, for income that varies, know your minimum amounts but use your average for the sake of this exercise.

Now for the second magic number, **your expenses** . . .

It takes a lot of money to run a life. Often we have expenses we don't even realize we're paying for, amounts we didn't realize were so high, and all kinds of crazy things happening in our bank accounts. But we're about to change that.

Log in to the bank accounts that detail your expenses and look at the transactions. Jot down your expenses for each of these line items:

- Housing (rent and mortgage)
- Utilities (gas, electric, heat, water, trash, etc.)
- Cable/TV/internet
- Home phone/cell phone
- Groceries/Eating out
- Public transportation
- Auto (gas, repairs, parking, insurance, etc.)

- Entertainment/vacation
- Other discretionary (hobbies, personal care, etc.)
- Shopping and clothing
- Gifts/donations
- Student loans
- Auto loans
- Credit card payments
- Savings

Total this number to get your second magic number, your expenses. This is the amount you need every month to run your life.

Great, now you have both numbers—your income and your expenses. The third number, called your bottom line, is **your income minus your expenses**. Whether that's a negative number or a positive number right now, take note because this number will determine the decisions you make in the pages ahead.

Bottom line: Your income minus your expenses

If your bottom line number is positive, you'll pull from it to reach your goals, such as paying off debt, investing, or buying a house. This positive number, whether $10, $100, or $10,000, is where you find wiggle room to start making decisions with your money.

If your bottom line number is negative, try not to get discouraged. When you're robbing Peter to pay Paul and running up an ever-increasing credit card balance, it can feel like there's absolutely no end in sight. But stick with me. There's so much wealth and beauty awaiting on the other side of this negativity, I promise.

If your bottom line is negative (or not at as positive as you'd like):

I want you to take two additional steps for me because we need this number to be positive. Want to know how to stay broke forever? Keep your expenses higher than your income. For some of you reading, this might be the case. Let's now take some steps so what's coming in is higher than what's going out.

Step #1: What expenses can you eliminate?

Here's what I want you to do. List the expenses you could potentially work on reducing. For example, perhaps you don't need to be paying for Disney+ and Hulu because you get them for free with your new cell phone plan. Or perhaps you didn't realize you were spending so much money getting takeout on your way home from your new job. If the expense is pushing you away from your goal to turn your bottom-line number positive and you feel like you can cut it down, put it on your list.

Before we get to the next step, I want to pause and address something that many financial books and experts don't. People are always saying, for example, to take the bus even if it means walking an hour to work. Who has time for all that? I want us to talk more about *making* money rather than focusing exclusively on how to limit spending it.

Step #2: How can you make more money?

To that point, now list all the possible ways you could create additional income. We have an entire chapter devoted to this topic, so for now let's just be creative with our brainstorming. Here are some questions to get you thinking:

- What skills or interests do you have that you could charge for? Maybe you play the piano and could teach young kids lessons. Or perhaps you love dogs and have a lunch break to walk your neighbor's puppy.

- Are there any assets you could rent or lease (like an extra bedroom to Vrbo or your car to a car-sharing app)?
- Is there any room in your current job to ask for a raise or could you pursue employment with another company willing to hire you for more money?

If you're wondering how all of this comes together, take a look at my community member Jacqueline's process of working through these steps.

JACQUELINE'S TWO MAGIC NUMBERS

INCOME/month	EXPENSES/month
Administrative assistant at a local security company: $3,604/month	• Housing (rent and mortgage): $1,100
	• Utilities (gas, electric, heat, water, trash, etc.): $211
	• Cable/TV/internet: $75
	• Home phone/cell phone: $45
Personal training on the weekends: averages $820/month	• Groceries: $300
	• Eating out: $400
	• Public transportation: $30
	• Auto (gas, repairs, parking, insurance, etc.): $120
	• Entertainment/vacation: $290
	• Other discretionary (hobbies, personal care, etc.): $150
	• Shopping and clothing: $220
	• Gifts/donations: $50
	• Student loans: $130
	• Auto loans: $260
	• Credit card payments: $400
	• Savings: $400
Total Monthly Income: $4,424	Total Monthly Expenses: $4,181

Monthly income – monthly expenses = BOTTOM LINE: $243

Jacqueline has a *positive* bottom-line number of +$243, which is the discretionary money she can put to work building wealth without accumulating more debt.

Now that you know your magic numbers formula—your income minus your expenses—you know what you have to work with, which is your bottom line. This is when you get to start making moves.

When you review a snapshot of your monthly income and your monthly expenses, you're aware and on top of exactly where you are, helping you to get to your goals more quickly. Feedback is information and information is what you need to make different decisions. For example, maybe you're trying to pay down $10,000 of credit card debt and you're feeling really good about the $400 you put toward it the last couple of months. If you're not looking at your numbers, you might not see that you have barely budged on that $10,000 (because, ugh, interest on the remaining balance adds up) and would say yes to that birthday trip even though you cannot afford it. Or, if your goal is to save $60,000 for a down payment in two years but you've only saved $4,000 in year one, you might need to skip that annual vacation or raise your prices if you're a business owner. If you're not looking at this stuff for six months, you won't be able to pivot in time to make the necessary changes. Time is money, after all!

Looking at my numbers every day, I see immediately when I spent too much on things that weren't important to me. Maybe last month I went out of town and shopped more than I should have. I know that wealth for me is so much more than buying recklessly, and that there has to be balance in order to protect what really matters to me, like my girls' education and a luxurious trip to a new country with my whole family, rather than a few new jumpsuits from Fendi. These numbers keep me moving toward my purpose of having wealth to begin with and keep me feeling in control.

Awareness over these numbers—what's coming in and what's going out—also gives you power over your transactions. For example, I took some clothes back to Intermix the other day. I wanted to make sure those items were credited back to my account, right? Or maybe I was charged twice at a restaurant. Those little catches add up and they happen all the time. Keeping tabs on your numbers means you're able to lock in financial wins for yourself at every turn. It informs your thinking, motivates your actions, and helps you make educated changes. I suggest these resources for taking inventory of your numbers and tracking them:

- Personal Capital—an online financial advising platform with a killer app that's a wealth manager at your fingertips.
- Mint—an easy-to-use app that gives you a clear picture of your overall financial situation and credit.
- YNAB (You Need a Budget)—a personal budgeting program.
- Many bank apps have built-in trackers, too!

Know Your Net Worth

As we talked about previously, feeling wealthy doesn't always come from a number. Feeling wealthy as a part of purposeful lifestyle design doesn't have to be born from a dollar sign at all. It can come from waking up next to someone you love, being in good health, or sitting on your porch . . . the little things. However, financial wealth is one way to bring your ideal lifestyle to fruition and enable your dreams. Part of knowing your numbers is understanding how to track the wealth you're building. There's one number that helps you do that, which is **your net worth**.

Many of the clients I've worked with in the past had no knowledge of their net worth. They had never calculated it. In fact, I had one client who sought financial advice. She came to me worried that her finances weren't doing that well. She didn't feel like she had saved as much as she should have, and she wanted guidance on how to start building wealth. We took inventory of her finances, which were distributed in normal places like checking and savings accounts, a Thrift Savings Plan (or TSP; a federal government retirement plan), and a couple of houses. Between the equity in these homes, the retirement account, and her savings, we realized that she already had the net worth of a millionaire. The client had no clue she was worth that much because she'd only been looking at the number in her savings account. I sat on the phone with her as she cried with relief. I felt like Oprah that day!

This is a unique situation, and I'm not saying you're going to calculate your net worth and suddenly realize you're a millionaire. But you will be able to focus on the total picture, good or bad. Maybe you've been superobsessed with your credit card debt and haven't looked at much else, including the 401(k) from your employer that makes your net worth positive. Or maybe you're feeling confident because you've been faithfully contributing to your retirement account for years but have lost track of major medical bills you've owed. Either way, you can't decide you're "not doing well" or "killing it" until you actually know the status of your net worth.

So how do you calculate your net worth? Fortunately, it's pretty simple. Your net worth is your total assets minus your total liabilities, or debts. Let's break down exactly how to do this, and remember, you can jot down all your personal numbers in the chart on page 79 or in the writable worksheet we have waiting for you at the QR code in the back of the book.

Let's first talk about your financial assets, or everything you have that holds value. Here are some examples:

- Checking accounts
- Savings accounts
- Investment accounts
- Retirement accounts
- Home value, if you own it
- Car value, if you own it
- Valuables
- Art
- Other real estate value

You total up these numbers and, *boom*, that is your list of assets.

Now add up your debts or anything that would potentially offset an asset. Debts include things like:

- Credit card balances
- Student loans
- Mortgages
- Car notes
- Medical bills
- Collections
- Other money owed

Once you total these numbers, you subtract your debts from your assets and, *boom*, you have your **net worth**.

YOUR NET WORTH

ASSETS	LIABILITIES
Checking account:	Credit card balance:
Checking account:	Credit card balance:
Checking account:	Credit card balance:
Savings account:	Credit card balance:
Savings account:	Student loan:
Savings account:	Student loan:
Investment account:	Student loan:
Investment account:	Student loan:
Investment account:	Mortgage:
Retirement account:	Mortgage:
Retirement account:	Car note:
Retirement account:	Car note:
Home value, if you own it:	Medical bill:
Car value, if you own it:	Medical bill:
Valuables:	Medical bill:
Art:	Collection:
Other real estate value:	Collection:
	Other money owed:
	Other money owed:
	Other money owed:
Assets total: $	Liabilities total: $

Your net worth (assets minus liabilities): $

Let's revisit our friend Jacqueline to see how her numbers looked.

ASSETS	LIABILITIES
Checking: $590	Credit card: $1,700
Savings: $9,855	Student loan: $33,000
401(k): $16,022	Car note: $19,985
	Medical bill: $250
Assets total: $26,467	Liabilities total: $54,935

Jacqueline's net worth: –$28,468

I did this exercise as I was working my way out of financial ruin. Because I owned a home (the one I was about to lose with late condo fees), the value of that home barely offset everything that I owed. So technically, I had a positive net worth. It might have been $1,000, but even to see that was encouraging. I needed that small win at a time when everything felt scary and bleak.

So, if your net worth is majorly negative or barely positive and you're freaking out over it, it really is not a big deal. Honestly. Let this be a motivating factor—it may be where you are today, but it's not where you're trying to stay. We're going to pay down those debts together soon and you'll start accumulating wealth and moving the needle on your net worth. So, if your magic numbers come out negative, or your net worth comes out negative as Jacqueline's did, realize it's just a starting point. It's not where you'll end up.

Your goal is obviously to make your net worth go up, and you can do this by saving and investing money, and by paying off debt. This will happen in three stages, which I call the foundational stage, the discovery stage, and the gathering stage.

The **foundational stage** is about growing your awareness. Everything we're doing in this chapter is part of building your foundation. You're understanding your numbers. This is the stage where we pay down debts, ramp up emergency savings, and start to build credit.

Next up is the **discovery stage**, where you determine your goals more specifically. Now that you're out of survival mode and into exploration, things are a bit more fun. You're learning what you want to build toward and experience the excitement growth can bring.

Last, you move into the **gathering stage**. You're distributing your money in different places—whether that's investments, retirement, real estate, or businesses. This is where you start thinking about generational wealth and how what you're building will impact the people who will follow you. You are living in abundance and your money has allowed you to create the life you've imagined for yourself and your family.

As you saw, our friend Jacqueline was in the foundational stage and was not too happy with her negative net worth. She took a deep breath and decided to make it positive within one year. Here's how she did it.

JACQUELINE'S NEXT STEPS

- Goal: she'd like her net worth to be positive within one year.
- To get there she's going to:
  - Eliminate things she doesn't need, such as a few recurring subscriptions, without going too bare-bones because she's not a lavish spender.
  - Sell her car to pay off the auto loan—because she walks everywhere anyway, including to her full-time job and her side hustle.
  - Talk to her boss about working half days on Fridays so she can take extra personal training clients those afternoons.
  - Raise her personal training fees.

Let's see how these small actions change Jacqueline's two magic numbers and her net worth:

JACQUELINE'S *NEW* TWO MAGIC NUMBERS

INCOME/month	EXPENSES/month
Administrative assistant at a local security company: $3,604/month	• Housing (rent and mortgage): $1,100
	• Utilities (gas, electric, heat, water, trash, etc.): $211
Personal training on the weekends: averages $1,120/month	• Cable/TV/internet: $65
	• Home phone/cell phone: $40
	• Groceries: $300
	• Eating out: $400
	• Public transportation: $160
	• Auto (gas, repairs, parking, insurance, etc.): $0
	• Entertainment/vacation: $290
	• Other discretionary (hobbies, personal care, etc: $140
	• Shopping and clothing: $220
	• Gifts/donations: $50
	• Student loans: $130
	• Auto loans: $0
	• Credit card payments: $400
	• Savings: $400
Total Monthly Income: $4,724	**Total Monthly Expenses: $3,906**

Monthly income – monthly expenses = BOTTOM LINE: $818

Jacqueline now has a *positive* bottom-line number of +$818, which she can use to pay down her credit card payment quickly, add to her savings, and begin to invest. Let's see how it impacted her net worth six months after implementing a few small changes:

ASSETS	LIABILITIES	
401(k): $16,022	Student loan: $33,000	
Savings: $11,459	Credit card: $0	
Checking: $2,194	Medical bill: $250	
	Car note: $0	
Assets total: $29,675	Liabilities total: $33,250	

Jacqueline's net worth: −$3,575

Jacqueline took her net worth from −$28,468 to −$3,575 (so much closer to a positive!) by analyzing her numbers and making changes in line with her lifestyle and her goals. You can take steps like these, too, even though the details will be unique to your circumstances. Yes, there are systemic challenges that keep rich people rich and poor people poor, but we're going to find the loopholes together. As we've talked about, most people are kept out of wealth because they lack access to knowledge, and I'm here to make sure that doesn't happen to you. We're going to get through it all together.

Four Net Worth Milestones

Knowing your net worth is a stepping-stone to many decisions you'll make next. There's no right, wrong, good, or bad goal for your net worth. It's entirely personal. Some people want to live comfortably in retirement, and that's all they need. Others want to live abundantly, or always having more than enough, now and forever, so they might be working toward a much larger net worth. Generally, I recommend setting milestones to reach a net worth that aligns with your lifestyle design. A straightforward first goal? Get into the positive with your net worth. Perhaps start with $10,000 and increase to $20,000 and then $50,000. As long as you're achieving your goals, keep raising the bar and keeping up the momentum!

Let's finish this chapter by creating four net worth milestones. Ask yourself the following questions and write down your answers in the space provided:

What do I want my net worth to be in six months?

_____

What do I want my net worth to be in a year?

_____

What about in three years?

_____

And ten years?

_____

Milestones compel you to check your net worth consistently, to see how you're making progress. When you notice an upward trajectory, I hope you'll celebrate yourself. This was something I wish I'd been better about. When I hit my goal of $100,000 net worth free and clear, I moved on quickly to the next goal without much thought. To achieve my overall purpose of financial and time freedom, I had to get to $1 million in net worth. But each $100,000 should have been a celebration marker until I got to that first million, and you know what? I didn't acknowledge those wins in-between as much as I could have. Remind yourself that you're on an incredible journey here, and that you always take the time to honor how far you've come and pat yourself on the back.

Even finishing this chapter is a step worthy of celebration, because, hey, you know your numbers now! You've taken the time to calculate your bottom line by knowing your two magic numbers (money coming in versus money going out) and calculating your net worth (your assets minus your debts). Bravo to you for taking up the compass and map that will lead you to the treasure chest of your future wealth.

Luckily, we are not in the old days anymore and we have technology to make all of this easier. Remember that you can get all the worksheets and my most up-to-date resources and apps related to this chapter by scanning the QR code at the back of the book.

CHAPTER 6

Face Your Debt Monster

TO FACE YOUR DEBT MONSTER . . .

- Understand the psychology of debt.
- Take four steps to RIP debt.
- Tackle your credit.
- Borrow your way wealthy.

recently bought my daughter Dawsyn a little purse. She *loves* dressing like Mommy, so when I was browsing in Target and saw a cute little collab that Target did with FAO Schwarz, I snagged the "fashion fabulous pink play purse" without looking inside. Sure enough, not five minutes after she started wearing the purse, Dawsyn ran up and handed me the gold plastic credit card that came with it . . . and begged me to swipe it. While I'm pantomiming a swiping motion and she giggles in delight, I'm also thinking, *Damn, this is crazy*. She's three. Why are we encouraging kids to enter the debt cycle via high-interest credit cards?

Having children has helped me realize how early we start conditioning *children* to get into debt. We see happy associations with debt everywhere—little kids with fake credit cards, people dancing around in credit card commercials, and credit cards sent to us in celebratory envelopes like we've just won the lottery—all of which communicate that debt is harmless. But credit card debt has a downside that we never talk about. If you don't pay it off, it balloons quickly as the interest increases with each charge. And the balance you carry affects your credit score, which is a number that lenders use to evaluate how likely you are to pay a loan back on time.

Credit card debt is not the only type of liability we are uneducated about. Another one is education itself. Take college, for example. From the second you step on campus, banks bait you with credit card sign-ups, offering free T-shirts and prizes. When I went to school, we had Capital One on campus, and they were giving out checking accounts and credit cards simultaneously to people who hadn't even lived on their own for longer than a week. Not only did the bank give you the money to attend college, but now they're giving you the credit card to rack up debt as you spend your way through college. You've borrowed to be there via student loans and now you're officially in the debt matrix getting lines of credit to stay there, racking up debt. Yet no one realizes they're being monetized by banks through loan interest and fees as soon as they set foot on campus.

When I attended Bowie State University, my mom got me my first credit card. She was big on building credit history early so I could have a good credit score. Credit scores affect your life in big ways, such as your ability to get a better rate on a mortgage or how much money you can get on a line of credit. Part of this chapter is devoted to your credit score, so hold tight! I believe the limit for this first card was $1,000 and within a year, the limit was raised to $12,000. I had no job, okay? And my limit still got raised 12x. This was nuts. Like most college kids would, I started using the card to the limit. Forget the school food: I had a car so I would drive off campus and pull up to great meals and head to happy hour. Eat here, eat there—I was living it up on that credit card! I put most of the money I ever charged on that credit union card. I probably racked up $6,000 in *food*, y'all. And you know I wasn't paying it off every month. Years after college, I was still paying for the chicken strips I had freshman year.

That's exactly how debt can interfere with your dreams. Ain't nobody building wealth when they're paying off a chicken strip they ate freshman year, and yet that is exactly what plenty of people are doing. They're taking a laissez-faire attitude toward credit cards, believing that it's not "real money." Only it is, and there will be a rude awakening later when you realize that you spent more than you have. And every day you can't pay it back, that owed money increases.

I use credit cards differently now. It's night-and-day, really. I no longer believe that there's good debt or bad debt. What matters is how you use debt. Debt that you use to make more money in the future is worthwhile. That will pay off, whereas chicken strips will not.

We're going to spend much of this chapter talking about debt, and if that scares you, you aren't alone. But debt isn't as powerful, permanent, and scary as it might seem right now. In the last chapter, you did the hardest part . . . You faced it. You put your debt down on paper. You looked at it square in the face and acknowledged that it existed. Now that you know your numbers, you can understand what to do with them. So now let's look at some basics pertaining to debt.

What Is Debt?

Anytime you borrow money, you're accumulating debt. It's pretty simple and straightforward. The message that gets far more muddled, although it shouldn't, is what type of debt to use and why. Luckily, there are clear boundaries that can help you make decisions on what will work for you, and what won't.

Borrowing money to buy things that hold no value is a quick way to go into debt and stay there. I see people getting into debt all the time because they can't stop charging meals, travel, and shopping to their credit cards, even though they can't afford these things. Recall when I was in college and splurged on eating out when I didn't have a job. This type of credit card debt will really control you because it gains interest, costs more over time, and snowballs into other negative situations, like dropping your credit score, forcing you to get behind on other bills, and having to borrow more expensive money. It could even lead to bankruptcy.

With most credit cards, if you don't pay your balance in full each month (and especially if you only pay the minimum payment), you're charged interest. Interest rates can range from nothing to 35 percent or more. Let's look at how a $5,934 credit card balance (the average balance held by Americans[1] at the time of this writing) costs you at a 20 percent annual percentage rate (APR). First, a few terms to know . . . An APR is determined by the credit issuer. They decide what interest rate they want to charge and can increase it for an individual based on their credit history. It is calculated daily and compounds, or accumulates. So you are paying interest on the principal, plus whatever interest accumulated the day before. When saving, compound interest is great. When in debt, it's not. Note that many credit cards start on a reduced promotional APR for the first year. You might have 0 percent APR, and then once that promotional period is over, it goes up to 20 percent. Also, credit card rates are variable, so they can go up if the Federal Reserve (which is the central bank of the United States and often referred to as the Fed) increases interest rates, which impacts interest rates on everything from mortgages to credit cards. They'll always announce this publicly when it happens, which is a great reason to pay attention to what the Fed is doing. On this card, imagine you had six months at 0 percent APR and then 20 percent once that period was over:

- If you carry this balance for a year, you'll pay $607 in interest.
- If you carry this balance for two years, you'll pay $1,202 interest.
- If you carry this balance for five years, you'll pay $3,179 in interest.

Let's take my client Tiff, for example. She's a single, African American woman with no kids making $140,000 a year in Washington, DC. Because she didn't know her numbers, Tiff was consistently spending more than she made each month. Tiff had a friend in Dallas who'd just had her first baby, so Tiff hopped on a plane at the last minute to be there, buying lots of presents for the baby because she wanted to be generous during a major milestone in her friend's life. She had the most wonderful time with her bestie and the new baby and returned to DC with her heart full. Within a couple of weeks of the trip, however, Tiff was feeling lonely in her new city. When her friends from college mentioned that they were meeting in Aspen, Colorado, to ski, she didn't want to miss out. They let her stay in the house they had rented, so in return Tiff treated everyone to dinner—the kind with many, many bottles of wine. In her mind, there was nothing stopping her from spending, not with the plastic money in her hand.

But when Tiff's credit cards were maxed, she was forced to pull from her savings to pay them off. She figured it would be fine because she'd replace her savings later in the year. But then her car broke down, and the mechanic required cash. She had so little money to fix her car—which she absolutely needed to get to her job—that she took out a payday loan with 120 percent interest, digging herself into even more debt. It wasn't until the monster had grown so big and scary, causing Tiff all the panic that I've felt in my past and maybe you have, too, that she decided to face this thing. She came to me to look at what was really going on, and understand the choices she was making and why, so that she would never get herself in this situation again.

Even though credit cards got me (and Tiff) into a bad spot, **credit cards are not evil**, and neither is credit card debt. Like all other borrowed money, it's all about how you use it. Let's take my old credit card habits, for example, back when I was paying for cheeseburgers and chicken strips years after I'd purchased them. Credit cards are a four-week debt period. You can borrow that money within the span of four weeks, but the day you go past that you're paying crazy interest rates and exponentially expanding the cost of whatever you purchased.

Once upon a time, I let my debt cycle go far beyond four weeks until the 20 percent interest rates were making it hard to keep up with the monthly payments, much less pay the thing off in full. I had my credit cards maxed out, with no plan to get out of the situation. I thought of credit cards as something that would allow me to pay for whatever I couldn't afford at the moment, which was a mentality that was exacerbating my debt. I'm so glad I've finally learned that lines of credit aren't there for me to buy things that I wouldn't be able to purchase right now. Lines of credit are there for me to leverage other experiences and benefits and ultimately get more with my money than I would have otherwise, which we'll talk about later in this chapter.

The Psychology of Debt

If you've created a debt monster from borrowing money that you haven't paid back, the most important thing you can do right now is understand *how you got into this mess of a debt*. If you don't know *why* you ended up there, it won't matter if you know *how* to get out, because you'll just end up in the same place all over again. Take a moment to reflect on these questions and jot down your answers in the space provided:

**ASK YOURSELF THESE QUESTIONS TO UNDERSTAND
THE PSYCHOLOGY OF YOUR OWN DEBT**

Why do you think you have this debt monster? What happened?

_____

_____

What were you spending money on?

_____

_____

How long were you ignoring this debt, and why?

_____

_____

When Tiff examined the psychology behind her debt, she realized that she was so focused on showing up for her friends that she didn't take the time to look at her numbers to see if she could actually afford what she was putting on her credit card.

She couldn't. She was spending more than she made. The truth was, Washington, DC, had been lonely and Tiff wasn't making a lot of friends. The invitation to visit her girls in other cities was tempting. In her mind she was spending her money on what mattered most in life—relationships and generosity—without realizing how much it would cost her. She ignored the debt for six months without looking at her statements.

When I went into debt starting my business, I simply was not making enough money. I wasn't even overspending! Rather, I had brought my lifestyle down to the bare minimum to float my business. My business had all kinds of unexpected expenses, like setting up my limited liability company (LLC), creating marketing materials, and paying for services like website hosting. So, while I removed trips, going out, and new clothes, it still wasn't enough. Before I knew it, I had a credit card maxed out at $15,000 that I couldn't pay off because my consulting fees were not high enough.

If you look at the psychology behind debt, you'll see that people go into debt for all kinds of reasons. Everyone's answers to the three questions are different. Some causes of debt cannot be helped, such as death, medical issues, divorce, and unemployment. Other people go into debt because they're overspending and haven't looked at the triggers and obstacles that we reviewed previously in this book.

There's no shame in debt, whether you could have prevented going there or not. You don't deserve a bunch of slaps on the hand. It happens to all of us, sometimes for reasons we *can* control and sometimes for reasons that we *can't* control. Even if you couldn't control it, because someone died and you were left to unexpectedly support your household or because you lost a job that you thought was supersecure, your path out of debt will be the same—one step at a time. However, without knowing your situation and why you got there, you'll simply be in a cycle where debt snowballs. Instead I want you to get to a place where your wealth is growing, but first, we need a plan to get out of debt.

FOUR STEPS TO RIP DEBT

1. Know what you owe.
2. Negotiate with creditors and collection agencies.
3. Follow the microwave method to reduce debts.
4. Find extra dollars to apply toward your debt.

Step 1: Know What You Owe

The first step in our plan to say goodbye to your debt is to gather and review your outstanding liabilities. Review each statement to understand the balance you owe and the minimum payment. In the following table, write down who you owe (that is, the name of the account/creditor), the annual percentage rate (APR), which is the rate that is charged for borrowing, the balance, and the minimum payment. If you're not sure that you have all of your creditors listed, you can obtain a credit report (which we'll review in detail later in this chapter, but you can skip to page 103 now if you like) as a way to double-check. AnnualCreditReport.com will give you a free report.

Account/Creditor	APR	Balance	Minimum Payment

Step 2: Negotiate with Creditors and Collection Agencies

You can negotiate with creditors or debt collection agencies to reduce your payment if you pay right away, or break up the amount you owe into smaller chunks as part of a payment plan. Debt collection agencies are third parties that help collect debts owed to the original creditor. When your debt goes to collections, your credit score can be negatively impacted.

- Before talking to a creditor or collection agency, be clear with yourself about how much you can afford to pay, either in full or as part of a payment plan. The last thing you want is to agree to something you can't afford on the call, and then default on a payment plan. They won't be willing to work with you anymore if you do that.
- On the call, explain your financial situation and what you can and cannot afford to pay.
- Ask for documentation of whatever you agree to, whether that's a reduced amount paid right then or a payment plan.

For my debts that were already in collections, I made phone calls to the collection agencies to see if I could negotiate a lower payment if I paid right away. That helped lessen the debt that I owed and erased some of it from my credit report, too, which gave me a double boost of credit improvement and debts that were washed away. In other situations where the debt was in collections but was too high to pay at once, even at a reduced amount, I set up a payment plan.

Step 3: Follow the Microwave Method to Reduce Debt

In the case of unhelpful debt that needs to be cleared out immediately (that is, anything with a high interest rate or on the verge of going to collections because you've missed the payment, or in collections already), you have to think about how you're going to start paying off this debt right away. There are a few ways you can do this. You can pay off the debt with the highest interest rate first, or you could clear out a debt with the lowest balance so you can get rid of it immediately.

I'm a big fan of a combined approach that focuses on fast wins—the **microwave method**. I call it the microwave method because it provides you with instant gratification and satisfaction, just like a microwave. This approach focuses on the debt that is costing you the most first, acknowledging that when you're in debt, you want those quick wins. This strategy will give you the motivation to tackle those higher balances, or the ones that seem impossible to wrap your head around right now.

When my debt monster was biggest, I felt like if I could knock out some of my teeny debts, I would believe I was making progress. Then I could deal with some of the larger balances and interest rates. Even though some of those small amounts had no interest rates and a lot of my debt was already with collectors, I just wanted to get those people off my back because they wouldn't stop calling and were affecting my emotional health. So I knocked out those smaller ones—the Comcast bill, and medical bills that were $50 or $100. Let me tell you, it was a great feeling to go from ten creditors to six in a matter of a few weeks!

Step 4: Find Extra Dollars to Apply toward Your Debt

In order to RIP debt, you have to go back to your numbers and look at your spending plan. When you're evaluating those two magic numbers, once your fixed expenses are covered, for the amounts left over you need to decide how much you can allocate toward your debt and savings. I think it's important to be saving even while you're paying off debt because times are hard. You want to be putting money away even when you're knocking debts off so that your emergency fund, which is a type of savings that we'll talk about in the next chapter, is still making progress. Credit cards are not an emergency cushion. Your limit could get cut off or lowered at any time, which could put you in a terrible position that leads to dire options like 200 percent interest rate payday loans and a drowning cycle of debt that is hard to exit.

Let's say, based on your spending plan and your two magic numbers, that you can afford to pay $500 a month toward your debts, but you have two different debts to pay. You'd consider putting $400 toward the highest-interest-rate debt, and $100 toward the smaller one in collections. So, you're still making the minimum payments, but you're putting a larger amount to whatever major debt you're tackling at the time.

Ultimately, you should figure out what works for you. I've seen plenty of people fail at paying debts because they were trying to do what worked for someone else. Let's say you have a crap ton of debt with superhigh interest rates that are costing you thousands of dollars a month. There's not a quick-win situation that makes any sense because you only have suffocating debt. There's nothing wrong with that; it's just the reality of your situation. You want to take that into consideration and figure out what a fast win with a big debt looks like. Maybe that's moving the debt or calling the credit card or loan company about moving or consolidating or lowering your rate, because another company offered you something lower and you're considering moving it. These are all options to you and can serve as examples of small but meaningful wins. Progress is what you're aiming for.

But don't try to cook a turkey in the microwave.

Let's talk about alternative options if chipping away at your debt with the microwave method isn't going to do the trick. If you have high-interest debts, the money you're able to put toward them might not make a dent. Consider these options instead.

Option 1: Initiate a balance transfer. This strategy entails moving one or many existing balances to another card with a much lower interest rate. Sometimes this can be beneficial, because if your balance is currently on a card with a 20 percent interest rate and you move it to a card with a 2 percent rate, the money you're saving can go directly to paying off the debt on the card.

If you go this route, you'll want to look for a small (or zero) balance transfer fee. Here's why. Let's say you initiate a balance transfer to a card with a much lower interest rate (2 percent on the new card instead of 20 percent on your current card). If you're paying a 10 percent balance transfer fee on top of that as a one-time payment, it's possible that you're not actually saving money. So, look for a balance transfer fee and any other fees you'd have to pay. Make sure you have a clear understanding of the terms (including how long the new rate lasts), and then run the numbers. Don't forget to stop using that old card. I see so many people initiate a balance transfer, move the balance, and then start running up the old card, too—making the debts even worse. Don't do that.

Option 2: Consider a debt consolidation loan. The purpose of this type of loan is to get all of your debt into one place with an overall lower interest rate than you would have paid with all the debts in various places.

Often, when you're in debt, you'll get offers in the mail for debt consolidation loans and/or balance transfers. Your job is to run the numbers and consider your options. You want to look for a loan that will save you money in the long run. Additionally, it's best if these loans only do a soft pull on your credit report versus a hard pull, because a hard pull goes onto your credit report. We'll dive into why that matters later in this chapter. More important, pick a debt consolidation loan that gives you a healthy amount of time to pay back your loan. If the repayment time frame is shorter but the interest on the loan is lower, versus a longer time frame with higher interest, ultimately you'll need to decide which monthly payment amount best fits your budget. Last, look for terms that allow you to keep your credit cards open. Some debt consolidation loans will force you to close all your credit cards, which would negatively impact your credit score because it reduces your available credit and can remove your credit history, making it hard to recover from in the near term. Don't worry, we'll be covering all things credit here shortly.

Believe it or not, you have options. Your debt isn't here to stay forever and ever . . . as long as you take your head out of the sand. Only then will you feel more in control because you'll know what's actually going on.

Now that you've faced your debt monster, it's time to befriend her. Because debt doesn't always have to snowball into something terrible.

Tackle Your Credit

Getting out of debt by facing that not-so-scary-anymore monster improves something else, too: your credit score. A credit score is a three-digit rating of how likely you are to pay back a line of credit. It's an indicator of your creditworthiness and dictates if you can get a loan of any kind—auto, mortgage, credit card, etc.—and what your interest rate will be. The better your score, the lower your interest rate in most cases. However, what many people don't realize is that your credit score is used in all kinds of ways, even sometimes when you're applying for a job. I've had friends, especially ones working in the federal government, who have not gotten a position because their credit wasn't good.

Your credit score is also used when you look for housing. Even if you can afford the house, you may not be able to live there if your credit score is too low. This just happened to my dad. He wanted to move into a certain community, and even though he had enough money to buy the home, the community had a credit score requirement and his did not pass. From mortgages to business loans to credit cards to investing, you can get stopped in your tracks by a low credit score. Banks and communities, and employers, use your credit score to determine whether you are responsible with money and can be trusted to pay what you owe.

Going broke can kill your credit score, which I like to think of as your adult GPA. I should know. Between debt collectors and closed bank accounts to unpaid credit cards and a repossessed car and an almost-foreclosed house, my credit was *not* in a good place. Even after I became a millionaire, I was still dealing with this because your credit report operates on seven-year cycles. Things stay on there, unless you can get them removed, for *seven* years. It's messed up, and I know people are trying to change the system because it's pretty hard to escape past mistakes, but for now that's the way it is.

When I first moved to Miami and was looking for housing, my broke years were way behind me. I was making incredible money with a solid business, yet even getting an apartment at the time required jumping through hoops. Because of negative marks on my credit report from late payments on my credit cards, mortgage, and debts in collection, the property made me put down an entire month's rent as a deposit instead of the first and last week, like they required of most people. Even now, when I am completely out of debt and have plenty of money, my credit score is haunting me. My score is in the high 700s (I'll be over 800 by the time this book comes out because the negative marks from that broke period of my life will *finally* have fallen off). But recently when I was buying a new house, the lenders were giving me a hard time about late pays on my mortgage back when I was broke, which theoretically could have stopped me from purchasing a home *seven years later, when I was a multimillionaire with a great credit score.*

I share this not to scare you, but to encourage you to take your credit seriously and tackle the little things that are in your control. I want to go over the basics because banks profit from your *not* knowing. The poorer your score, the more interest they can charge and thus the more money they make from you. Let's look more closely at how the interest situation works and why a low credit score ends up costing you a lot of money.

If your score is low (let's say 500), it means that when people are determining your creditworthiness, they believe it's riskier to lend money to you. Because of that, they'll charge more to lend that money to you than they would to lend it to someone who has a high 700. This makes sense. After all, the person with a 700 has a proven track record of paying bills on time.

So when people ignore their credit score, sometimes they're surprised by the interest rate when they try to do something big like buy a house. Let's say a mortgage broker would have given them a 4 percent interest rate, but because of their credit score of 500, the interest rate is 8 percent. If you factor that over a 15- or 30-year loan on a mortgage, that can equate to hundreds of thousands of dollars. Same thing with cars. I've worked with people who have gotten the crappiest deals on cars, driving a really inexpensive vehicle but paying $800 a month for it because their interest rate is so high. This means they're paying substantially more for a car than it's even worth. It's hard to stomach, especially when a car might be nonnegotiable for work, but this is the type of thing that your credit score can totally screw you on, costing you tens of thousands of dollars on a simple auto loan.

I've even seen people's credit scores prevent them from opening bank accounts. There's a system that banks use called the ChexSystems, which is like your credit score within the banking world. It's used to identify the people who open a bank account, run it negative by one, two, three thousand dollars, leave it, and then open another account somewhere else and run this one negative, too. Between all these banks and negative bank accounts, the person has raked in thousands of dollars in debt they'll never pay back. It makes sense that creditors would want to keep an eye out for those people.

Even in less extreme cases, if you bounced a check, mismanaged your funds, overdrafted, or experienced fraud, your bank might report it, which will affect your ChexSystems score and may prevent you from opening another bank account. You might use something called second-chance banking in the interim, where a second-tier bank will take on a low credit score or ChexSystems score customer subject to a deposit and/or certain limitations.

The bottom line? These scores aren't something to take lightly. Your credit significantly impacts how quickly you can build wealth. Luckily, there are many things you can do to make your credit score work for you. Let's start with the main things you need to know about credit reports.

Who generates credit reports? Credit bureaus are essentially data collection agencies that aggregate information about your credit history and sell it to lenders, which is any financial institution, group, or individual that makes money available to a borrower and expects it to be repaid, usually with interest. The three bureaus—Equifax, TransUnion, and Experian—gather and package your data to tell banks and lenders if you're a good girl or bad boy. They also sell your information to other people in the form of a credit report. They each generate different reports and you can have different scores, information, errors, and discrepancies depending on which one you consult, so you'll want to keep tabs on all three.

What is the credit score range? This changes from time to time, but currently the range is 300–850 for scores given from the three main bureaus, Equifax, TransUnion, and Experian. If you hear other scores, like FICO scores and Vantage scores, understand that these are brands of scores with their own unique numerical weighting system based on information that they've gathered from all three agencies. They're basically the same as your credit score because they measure the same thing, just with a different scoring model.[2]

What are credit inquiries? You can look at your credit score from any of these credit bureaus as much as you want without impacting your credit score. However, if you have a *hard pull* on your credit report, it goes onto your report. A *soft pull* will not. A hard pull occurs when you give a financial institution permission to use your personal information to perform a credit check for a loan or some other line of credit. A hard pull takes a deep look at the items on your credit report so a lender can decide if a loan will be granted. A soft pull, on the other hand, reveals the same information, but it's used more as a background check (for example, if you're getting a job or signing a lease). Too many hard pulls on your credit in a short amount of time negatively affect your credit score because it looks like you're in desperate need of money and thus at a higher risk to default on the loan. Soft pulls do not impact your credit score. When credit checks come up—whether you're applying for a loan, a lease, a job, or an investment—ask whether the person is doing a hard or soft inquiry.

Where do I get my credit report? You can go directly to either Equifax, TransUnion, or Experian, or we have resources available at the QR code in the back that pull information for you. Remember, checking your own credit report is always a soft pull!

How do I read my report? I'm so glad you asked. Every report contains slightly different information depending on what you pull (something from the credit bureaus, something automated from a finance app, or a FICO/Vantage/private scoring company, etc.). Let's walk through the main details to look for on your credit report, which are weighted to arrive at your final score.

Accounts and Outstanding Balances: You should see a breakdown of each of your credit accounts—home loans, student loans, auto loans, credit cards, etc.—detailing the limits and your outstanding balances. If there are credit limits, you should see how much of the credit line you're currently using up, which weighs heavily (about 30 percent) into your credit score. It's a good idea to keep your credit usage as low as possible if you're trying to raise your score. When lenders are looking into your debt-to-income ratio, they're taking into account how much debt you're already committed to in comparison to how much money you're bringing in.

Length of Credit History: The length of time you've been building your credit matters to your overall score. The longer the history the better. Even a single credit card with a small limit, like a couple hundred dollars, is enough to begin building credit history.

Credit Inquiries: You'll see a list of the hard inquiries into your credit history and by whom. As I mentioned, having a lot of these inquiries on your credit report during a short amount of time can bring your overall score down and it's a red flag. When you are examining your credit report, this is a good time to make sure that you actually approved all those queries.

Payment History: You'll also see payments for each of your accounts and if they were paid on time or late. Late payments negatively impact your credit score, so if something was reported as late even though it wasn't, you should work with the lender in question to get that payment right-sized and reported correctly.

Identity and Accuracy: It likely goes without saying, but you should check each of these sections for accuracy. If you spot any errors, whether about payment history or accounts you never opened, you can and should dispute these errors to get them off your report. The easiest way is to pick up the phone and communicate with your lender. People often do not realize they can do this.

Your conversation can look something like this:

Hi, (insert bank of choice). I know from my credit report that you reported a late payment from me a couple years ago. As you can see, I have a strong history since then of paying my bill on time. Would you be able to take that off and send me documentation that confirms as much?

While you can reach out online, I recommend calling. By talking with them, you'll be better able to understand what the lender can do for you. Then you can take their written plan and submit it directly to the credit bureau to ensure you have your bases covered. You can use this same talk track with any lenders or collectors that might have submitted to the credit bureaus.

If you're wondering whether to go to the credit bureau or the lender first, that's a very common question. Many people will reach out to both about items on their credit report like late payments, personal information, or inaccurate lines of credit. However, you don't always need to do that. If, for example, you see a high-level error on your report, like your personal identity, address, or spouse, you'll want to reach out to the credit bureau to correct it immediately. When you reach out to the credit bureau directly, it's normally about something that was supposed to be changed or removed on a report but wasn't. On the other hand, when you have a detail edited on the lender's side, it's generally specific to you as the account holder and updates automatically on all three of the credit bureau reports.

Think about it this way. Imagine you received an incorrect grade on your report card. You wouldn't get that report card changed by the principal (the credit bureau in this case). You'd go to the teacher who graded the paper incorrectly (the lender). They're the one who submitted that mark to the principal's office, which in turn generated the report. Same goes here. You'll probably get most changes made by the lender that owns your account where the negative mark was reported from. Then, if they've done their end of the deal and it's still not getting fixed, you can work directly with the credit bureaus. Different situations will require work with different parties, either the lender or the bureaus themselves.

One last thing on this point: you might also investigate credit repair tools, or services that will help you with these things for free and for a premium. Companies are popping up to help you clean up your credit, but you can do this work yourself and save money simply by communicating with the lender that submitted the negative mark. When you're monitoring your own credit, you'll catch these things more quickly.

There are plenty of ways to monitor your credit, and you can see some of my current favorite tools at the QR code in the back, but it's most important to view each of your credit reports regularly. Even if you use a tool that gathers all of the information for you, you'll want to make sure that you're pulling the reports from each of the three bureaus to audit the details. As you now see, even the slightest change of information can have an impact on your score, which can save you money and help you on your wealth-building journey over time. Do all of it, especially if you know that you're nearing an important decision like getting a loan for an important life event. Your credit score weighs heavily during these times and you don't want to be surprised. You want to give yourself time to adjust discrepancies, repair your credit, and set yourself up for success for whatever next step in your journey is ahead! Improving your credit score, which will give you better interest rates than someone with a worse score, allows you to focus on the kind of debt that actually expands your wealth—a little something called *leverage*.

Borrowing Your Way Wealthy

Wealthy people realize that money makes money. But you can't get there if you're always in the wrong kind of debt. Leverage is an investment strategy in which you borrow money (debt) to make *more* money and increase your potential return. You're borrowing money to pay for something with value that will go up more quickly than the interest on the loan you took out. It's helping you accrue wealth, not go into a hole that feels impossible to get out of.

Leverage shows up in all kinds of ways, provided you're using borrowed money to your advantage. Real estate in general is a debt most people consider to be leverage because when the value of a home goes up, so does your net worth—or, if you decide to sell it, you've made more money than the home loan you took out to purchase the house initially. You're able to leverage the home to purchase other homes or get a business loan, since it's an asset. As another example, taking out loans for your business to pay for office space and new hires is leverage because it will allow you to expand in ways that will earn you more money in the long run. If borrowing money is going to ultimately make you money, you're leveraging.

Here are a few specific examples of how borrowing money can make you money:

Example 1: A Home

You purchase a $380,000 home by putting in $80,000 as a down payment and then got a mortgage for $300,000 to cover the balance. If you then sell the home for $525,000, you've leveraged your debt, because the money you used to purchase the home appreciated, earning you a return.

Example 2: The Stock Market

Let's say you borrow money that costs you 4 percent interest, but the stock market has average annual returns of 10 percent. If you're investing in the stock market, you're receiving higher returns on your money.

Example 3: A Car Loan

You take out a low-interest car loan for $45,000 as a business expense for your jewelry business because you're always driving around to markets to showcase and sell your product. You can use the cash you didn't hand over for the car to invest in marketing and expanding your staff, which will make your jewelry company even more money. That's leverage.

The flip side to this example: I see plenty of people losing money on the very same purchase that other people make money on, like a car loan. If you get a bad deal on an auto loan because your interest rate is so high, that means you're ultimately paying more for the car than the vehicle is worth. If you have a car loan for $20,000 but the car is worth only $15,000, that's a debt that isn't helping you; it's hurting you. You're losing money.

Sometimes it's leverage, sometimes it's not.

While credit cards that you don't pay off are a major contributor to your debt monster, once you have a handle on your debt and a good grip on your finances, it's time to start using credit cards to your advantage. Most cards have features and bonuses for certain purchases. For example, I use my American Express card for business expenses such as Facebook ads. Thanks to my Amex, I have access to a platinum lounge when I'm traveling that makes my experience infinitely better at the airport, providing a nice space to work and get things done when I'm waiting for my flight . . . and free old-fashioneds! I have multiple credit cards, and I pay off each one every month. Yes, I'm accumulating monthly debt, but it gets paid on time, so I'm only paying what I spent, not any compound interest, *and* I'm getting amazing benefits and perks by sending my money through that credit card. There are many cards out there that can help with everyday items. You want to look for those from major institutions that provide cash back or other benefits helpful to you.

Last year I accumulated 2.5 million points on that Amex, which I leveraged to take my family on a trip to Deer Valley resort in Utah. This trip would have cost me more than $15,000 if I had paid in cash. All my bills are routed to my cards because I can leverage those points to buy just about anything. I think about credit cards as straight-up leverage now. How can I use these cards to get as many points as possible to get free travel, free perks, free hotel stays, free airline tickets? You name it!

Remember, these cards do more than just get you perks; they also protect your purchases. If you order something that doesn't come, or there's fraud, most credit cards have your back. Take the time to read the fine print on credit cards to make sure that this is in fact the case, and make sure to utilize this benefit. Unlike when you use a debit card, it's very easy to recover your money if something goes wrong with a credit card purchase.

Many of you have been taught to stay away from credit cards at all costs, and that they're always bad. However, utilizing them in this way—once you've shooed away your debt monster and know why you got into debt in the first place—is part of building a positive relationship with debt. However, if you choose to spend money you don't have by racking up credit card bills, your credit cards are no longer being used as leverage.

Here's a different example of how leverage isn't always obvious. Most people would consider student loans to be "good debt," something that will make you more money in the long run and would thus be considered leverage. Historically, there are numbers to prove it. If you have a bachelor's degree, you earn 67 percent more than someone with a high school diploma, according to the US Bureau of Labor Statistics. In 2020, the rate of unemployment for those with bachelor's degrees was 5.5 percent while the unemployment rate for those with high school diplomas was 9 percent.[3] When taking the issue at face value, having a college degree puts you in a better financial position than someone who doesn't have one. More education also decreases rates of depression and anxiety and is associated with better health outcomes and lower mortality rates.[4] This is all superimportant when considering what it means to you to live a wealthy life.

Hold up, though. Here's what people gloss over. According to the Federal Reserve Bank of New York, 33.9 percent of all college graduates hold jobs that don't require a college degree. And 41.3 percent of *recent* graduates hold a job that doesn't require a college degree.[5] The cost of a four-year degree has nearly tripled since 1980, even when accounting for inflation. The typical undergraduate comes out of college with $25,000 in debt, according to analysis by the US Department of Education. And get this: almost one-third of borrowers have debt but no degree.[6]

These numbers disproportionately affect Black borrowers. Also, according to the White House Fact Sheet on Student Loan Relief, "Middle-class borrowers struggle with high monthly payments and ballooning balances that make it harder for them to build wealth, like buying homes, putting away money for retirement, and starting small businesses."

For some people, student loans are completely worth it. For others, they're not. Like all things in life, debt is what you make of it and student loans are no different. I went to college and got my bachelor's and my master's degrees. What I learned wasn't necessarily what I needed in my day-to-day job. But it gave me the "legitimacy" that the firms I wanted to join required. With the skyrocketing cost of higher education today, you really have to ask yourself if the return on your investment will be worth it.

Take Rae, who is a married mother of two and lives in Knoxville, Tennessee. She has $75,450 in college loans from a private university where she studied journalism. She wrote for various media outlets for a few years, but when her husband's job took them to Tennessee, she couldn't find work in her field and started a job as a virtual assistant instead. Rae did not need her journalism degree for this lower-earning role, and she is saddled with debt. Little did she know that mass media, an umbrella term for majors like journalism, broadcasting, and communications, has the highest unemployment rate of any major.[7] Not everyone needs to go to college and not all student loan debt is good debt, but we live in a society where a bachelor's degree is still the minimum prerequisite for most jobs. It's an unjust system that keeps people in debt. Simple as that.

I see so many people who go to school on borrowed money and

it becomes unhelpful debt. Maybe that's because they didn't finish school, or they didn't take advantage of the network from that school. Maybe they can't make a living wage with their major, or maybe they keep going to school, racking up college loans, with no line of sight on the profession that will help them pay this money back. I've seen my clients borrow money to go to trade school, then cosmetology school, then return for their bachelor's degree and then their master's degree and they are still not able to hold a job. Student loan debt, in these situations, is nothing more than a whole lot of debt they can't pay back. That's not leverage.

Student loan debt is a great example of debt that's not "all good" or "all bad." If you think about it, life is like this, too—not black-and-white but shades of gray. Not all bad debt represents bad decisions. Maybe you got a personal loan to handle a major health crisis. You're keeping yourself alive, so that's not a bad debt even if the interest rate is high! Or perhaps you carried a large balance on your credit card one month because your employer paid you late, which kept you from missing your rent. One could argue that was a good use of "bad debt." This isn't about justifying actions that hinder wealth, but I do want you to have compassion for the context in which debt is used.

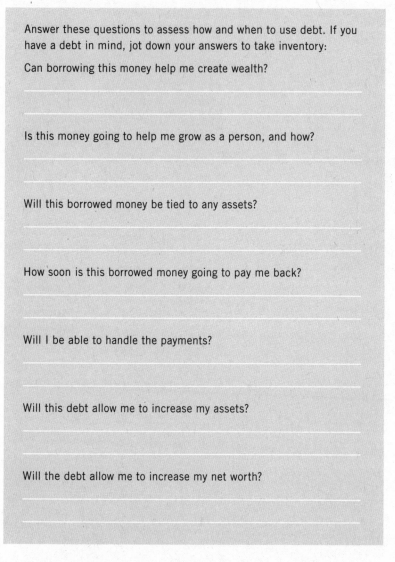

Answer these questions to assess how and when to use debt. If you have a debt in mind, jot down your answers to take inventory:

Can borrowing this money help me create wealth?

_____

_____

Is this money going to help me grow as a person, and how?

_____

_____

Will this borrowed money be tied to any assets?

_____

_____

How soon is this borrowed money going to pay me back?

_____

_____

Will I be able to handle the payments?

_____

_____

Will this debt allow me to increase my assets?

_____

_____

Will the debt allow me to increase my net worth?

_____

_____

People who build wealth understand when to use debt as leverage and when it's just becoming a debt monster. When debt is used for the right thing, for the right decisions, it's the right debt!

CHAPTER 7

Make Saving Simple and Sexy, Then Circulate Your Way to Wealth

FIVE STEPS TO SIMPLE AND SEXY SAVING

- Complete your four-step savings strategy.
- Choose your savings sweet spot.
- Use my three savings tricks to speed it up.
- Determine if you're circulating or spending.
- Review whether your dollars are doing their jobs.

Back in the days when creditors were ringing my phone off the hook, the only thing I was motivated enough to save for was my emergency fund. When I was barely making $40,000 a year, I was simply saving what I could. At the time, that was a few hundred dollars, which I would set and forget. Each month I could count on that money going in, but I also did something extra sneaky. I set up a recurring twenty bucks to go into my account every Thursday, because I knew I'd barely notice it and it would serve as a little boost to my savings. I did this because it can be hard to focus on saving when it feels like you're drowning, which back then . . . I was.

As my income increased, I focused on saving a few thousand dollars a month. Because I'm self-employed, I created a regular pay-myself-day on which I automatically put money into savings each month to create consistency. Housing costs were my biggest expense—as they are for most people—and my goal was to save as much as I paid in rent, which meant that I needed to find a place to live with a rent payment that did not take up all of my income. Slowly but surely, this allowed me to reach my intended monthly savings contribution.

I wanted to increase my savings to a year's worth of expenses—also known as my emergency savings—and to continue to elevate my net worth. At first the emergency fund was all I could focus on, until later savings became about retirement, investments, and other big-picture goals. Now that I'm a multimillionaire, my savings strategy is much more complicated, but starting with an amount that you can save comfortably and consistently is what matters most.

Look, saving isn't supposed to be hard. It's not supposed to be complicated. This should be the most straightforward chapter in this book if we're doing this right.

Savings gives you the ability to move. It gives you options, possibilities. You can fix a problem with money. You can travel. You can leave a marriage. You can get advanced medical treatments. You can have kids or not have kids. You can choose when and where and how you want to work. All of that starts with having savings that you can rely on. People don't just wake up and become millionaires. They start by tapping into their savings, which gives them the confidence to take different risks, make different decisions, and start building wealth with their money over and beyond their emergency reserves.

Saving is as simple as putting money aside for later. It's considered *saving* (versus *investing* or *leverage*) because this money isn't exposed to any risk. If you save it, it means that there's no chance you could lose that money. That's where it's different from investing. Investing means you don't just want money to sit there: you want it making money for you—even if that means being exposed to volatility in the market. These bigger risks often return an even higher reward. But for now, we're going to focus our efforts on the money *not* exposed to major risk, money that's available to you for an emergency, a business, or a goal that really matters to you, like buying a home.

You might be wondering *why* you should be saving to begin with. Imagine sitting on a stiff, hard-ass chair for an entire week while you're trying to get your work done. You'll probably end up in a lot of pain. The work won't flow. You'll be rigid and miserable. And it will just be *uncomfortable*. But then I come along and roll up this plush, ergonomic, luxury office chair for you to sit in. Suddenly your work becomes more enjoyable, your body hurts less, and you can get so much more done . . . just from a little cushion.

Saving for an emergency, at minimum, is like having a cushion that gives you financial independence. It's hard to convey how emotionally game changing it is to know that you have options. I remember my broke days when I was scared to leave the house because I had no emergency savings or safety net if something went wrong. If I got a flat tire, I wouldn't know what to do, because all of my credit cards were shut down and I'd have no way to pay. I had so little money to save me if something happened that I preferred to not do anything at all. That's no way to live—nervous, scared, and preparing for the worst.

Once I started building back my savings, my confidence came back. I felt more comfortable and free in the financial decisions I was making. I felt like I could start moving again, getting back out there, looking for moneymaking opportunities, and fully experiencing my life . . . because if anything happened, I could handle it.

And things have certainly happened. When I was eight months pregnant, I got very sick with COVID and ended up in the hospital. My then-partner also had COVID and had to be hospitalized. Once I tested negative, I was kept away from him in a quarantine room where I was served cold meals out of little plastic boxes. I had the baby in that hospital alone, and at the same time, they were telling me that my partner was on his last breaths. I'll save you the harrowing details, but let's just say everyone's life was at risk—mine, our newborn's, and my then-partner's. Thankfully, everyone fully recovered.

While I am (and was) the primary breadwinner, both of us were unable to work for many months. It was totally unexpected and scary. Luckily, I had the savings to get us the best doctors. (The same cannot be said of the way we were treated at the hospital, but we'll save my hot take on the health care system for another book. TL;DR: I'm going to buy that hospital one day so no Black person has to ever experience what we experienced.) We weren't financially ruined, but we could have been if we didn't have my savings. If you want to be able to do whatever the hell you want to do, think of savings as your way to have complete control.

Money isn't the answer to all of life's problems, but it can be a solution to many if you have it, know how to use it, and know why you're saving it. I see plenty of people with absolutely no desire to save their money, which normally manifests a few ways:

Some people think savings will just happen. Many of my clients figure they'll wait until the end of the month to see what's left to save. If you do that, I can promise you that most of the time, there won't be anything left. Here's my golden rule: start saving first, before you spend. This advice has stood the test of time because it's true. Nothing is guaranteed about saving money unless you do the work of saving it.

Some people think there's no reason to save. Whether they're worried about another pandemic or global warming, or they're not planning on having kids, some people are bleak about the future and thus they don't see the point in saving. They feel like they're not guaranteed to be alive three weeks from now, so why save for thirty years from now? But I always say, why not plan for the best-case scenario? Why not architect your life and your savings so that when humanity does figure it out, when you do get gray hair, you're having a great time and it's worth it?

Some people don't feel like they have enough money to save. It can be easy to look at all of your debts and feel like what you are saving is hardly making a dent. However, this won't be the case forever. Eventually your debts will be paid off and you can go from making nominal contributions to your savings account to bigger ones. Everyone has something that can be saved, even if that's mere dollars you forgot were sitting in your Cash App. However, if you don't get into a mindset of prioritizing savings now, it won't happen later just because you're making more money. Savings needs to be valued no matter what financial situation you're in.

Some people want everything perfect before they start saving. If you're waiting for everything in your financial future to be perfect—making enough money, paying off all your debts, etc.—before you start saving, you'll never get there. You're planning for the future and making it better with your choices today, not waiting for that future to be all buttoned up before you start thinking about these things. It really does start right now, ready or not.

Some people save it, but *don't* forget it. Remember that broke-millionaire environment we talked about in the chapter on our money origin stories? I see people saving all their money for something big, let's call it a house, and then blowing it all in one fell swoop, emergency savings and all. Then, when something happens (maybe their car dies), they're house poor and go into debt because they didn't truly know their numbers or understand the value of having money saved no matter what. We're not saving money to spend *all* of it. Some money is only meant to be spent in emergencies.

If you've never had wealth, or even a little extra money, it can be difficult to see how life changing saving money can be for your well-being. It might seem like nominal amounts you're putting aside right now, but money adds up. However, it never will if you don't save it, which is why you have to start somewhere, today.

YOUR FOUR-STEP SAVINGS STRATEGY

Let's now set your savings strategy across the short term, the medium term, and the long term. Your saving strategy is made up of four crucial factors: 1) exactly how much you have to save, 2) the goal you're saving toward, 3) the amounts and frequency you will save, and 4) your savings accountability partner.

Step 1: Decide exactly how much you have to save.

As a general rule, save 10–20 percent of your income after taxes. But ultimately, you have to look at your number from the previous chapter to determine if you can indeed save that much without going into debt. If you can't, calibrate your numbers until you can. It's okay if the amount is lower as long as you're making progress on your net worth by using your money to pay down debts.

Step 2: Determine the goal you're saving toward.

As I've alluded to, everyone should have a nonnegotiable emergency fund, which is ideally housed in an easily accessible account with no penalties for withdrawing money—such as a high-yield savings account. This account serves as a cushion for emergencies and can cover up to nine months of expenses. Beyond this, though, you want to set up a goals-based savings account. This is for whatever else you've decided that you're saving for. Whether that's extra runway for a rainy day, a sabbatical, a business investment, or home renovations—it's up to you. Decide how much you'll need to save so you know exactly what needs to be done over the coming months and years.

Step 3: Decide the amounts and frequency at which you will save.
Determine the amount of money you need to put away and for how long. The amount is based on your monthly budget. When you look back at your two magic numbers, what are you able to save? That amount can then be divided based on your pay period, which gives you your savings frequency. This could be as simple as $100 every two weeks for two years. Or it could be $1,000 a month for six months. This number is up to you and should be determined in accordance with your overall spending plan and the availability of funds.

Step 4: Identify a savings accountability partner.
Putting money away, especially if you're not a natural saver, can be supported by having people in your corner who are there to encourage you toward your goals. Just like anything else that benefits from an accountability partner, savings goals are no different. Determine how often you'll check in with this person and set your calendar accordingly. Pick someone you can be honest with, and who you know is invested in your dreams. This could be a family member, a partner, a friend, or a colleague. Anyone who is in your wealth corner!

Now drop everything and complete these four steps.

Choose Your Savings Sweet Spot

Even after I've provided the 10–20 percent range, everyone always asks me exactly how much they should be saving. I wish I could give you an exact number. If you google how much to save, you'll find a lot of suggestions about what percent of your after-tax money should be squirreled away. If you do the same for emergency savings, you'll find anything ranging from two months to two years. I share this because the 10–20 percent range is based on best practices from my former career as a licensed financial planner, and now as someone who talks, studies, and thinks about personal finance 100 percent of the time. But you should also take a step back and look at your expenses to determine how much you can realistically put away. Remember, even if your two magic numbers landed you in the negative, I still want you putting *something* into your emergency savings while you're paying off your debts. Ideally, I want your first savings goal or sweet spot to be 10 percent of your income. From there, you can move that number up.

When it comes to emergency savings, five years ago I would have told you to have three to six months of expenses saved. Now I'll say that it should be closer to nine months. Why? Well, the world has changed. We've seen how quickly a pandemic can shut down the global economy. We've seen what can happen to a job market in an instant, and how long it can all last. I want you to be prepared for these things. Now, when I talk about your expenses, I'm referring to your basics, or everything you need to live if you lose your moneymaking ability tomorrow. This might mean you're living a bare-bones life to make your savings go as far as possible. However, some of you may want your emergency fund to reflect your current lifestyle. That's fine, too. It's your choice to decide what months of expenses mean for you.

As I said earlier, you want to be saving first, before anything else gets spent or allocated. It should be the very first money that goes out, because it's going to you. We'll talk about automation in a moment, but in an ideal world, 10–20 percent of your after-tax income should be going to savings. First, that money will go to your emergency savings if that fund is not where it needs to be. Next, it should go to a savings account set aside for your other goals, whether that's buying a house or going on a big trip. Eventually those monies will be allocated to investments, depending on your risk profile.

I'm currently at an 80 percent savings rate and many of my community members are at 50 percent. It really depends on the money you have available to put away. For most people, though, a comfortable sweet spot is 10–20 percent of your after-tax money, particularly because you might be simultaneously saving for retirement (which often automatically comes out of your paycheck).

My savings rate has changed many times over the years, and it has always been based on what I could afford. This is important. You wouldn't believe the number of people I've seen over the years who are saving their way into debt, overshooting their savings sweet spot. I know it sounds counterintuitive, but it happens all the time. When people aren't paying attention to their numbers, they put far more into retirement, investments, and emergency savings than they can actually afford, and they don't leave themselves with enough money to manage their everyday expenses. This means that they either end up pulling money out of their savings to live, pulling money out of retirement accounts (thus facing a heavy tax bill or early withdrawal penalties), or putting expenses on high-interest credit cards. If you get into an oversaving cycle, you end up having plenty of money saved but nothing to show for it because your net worth hasn't budged. When determining your savings sweet spot, it's better to save what you can afford and *not* go into debt than to save a ton but rack up high-interest debts in other places.

Three Savings Tricks to Speed Things Up

With a plan, anything is possible. However, there are strategies that make your dreams even easier to achieve. No one hits their goals in an instant or because they read one book or completed a worksheet. Getting my debts cleared, my emergency savings back, and my wealth built took years, but it happened one decision at a time. So, I want to let you in on a few savings tricks that I learned over the long run, which you can hopefully implement sooner to speed up your journey.

Automate everything. Create a recurring payment through your bank or from your paycheck for whatever you want to save. When you automate your savings, you can set the date for the money to be withdrawn when you receive your paycheck. That money then automatically goes into your savings or investment accounts. Set it and forget it! It's one decision you've made that will continue to pay into your dreams. The fewer decisions you have to make, or actions you need to take, especially if you're tempted to spend your savings, the closer you will be to your wealth goal.

Choose your savings account wisely. You want your savings to go to a place that is accessible should you need it in an emergency, but not so accessible that you can move your money at a moment's notice. I suggest setting up emergency and goal-based savings accounts with a separate banking institution from your regular checking account. You can access these with a card that you don't keep handy in your wallet. As I mentioned, look for a high-yield savings account so that the money inside is making money while you're not touching it. One to 2 percent interest rates on these accounts is better than nothing.

Turn your sacrifices into savings wins. Saying no to Beyoncé tickets is admittedly difficult. Even if I "couldn't afford" to buy Beyoncé tickets, if they were available to me I'd probably find a way to pay for them. I don't believe you have to sacrifice your way to wealth. You can have that damn $5 latte. You can see your friends. And you can still save. Here's a trick I've found useful. When you *do* say no to something—maybe it's the girls' dinner you turned down because you just saw your pals two nights ago—take the $100 you would have spent and transfer that money into savings. If every time you are about to spend money, but decide against it and instead save that money, you're turning your nos into yeses, flexing the muscle of decision making and also of building your savings.

I hope this part of the chapter has your savings wheels turning. Saving is important not only to your financial success, but also to your well-being. Having savings reduces your stress, improves your health,[1] and allows you to move freely because you have more choices. It's an unbelievable feeling to know you have options, and options start with creating, maintaining, and succeeding at your savings plan. Once you have your foundation secure, circulating your way to wealth becomes all the more important. Let me explain.

When you circulate your money, this means it will eventually be returned to you in one way or another. Even when I'm spending $40 on barbecue, I'm thinking about how I put that money into the city of Miami, where I live. I'm supporting a small business, which is great karma for *my* business. On top of that, the food provides my family with nutrition. I put this money out there and it comes back to me as a benefit in another form.

Whether you're spending money on gas or paying your taxes or buying a coffee, you can either see this money as being spent, done and gone, or you can see it as bringing something back to you that you need. Now, this mindset of circulation isn't meant to justify spending that leads to debt. Circulating money needs to have purpose. Let's take the money you spend on coffee as an example. If caffeine puts you in a better mood and makes you more productive to get your work done, then circulating that money here makes sense. The coffee is giving you the fuel you need to make your money, versus skipping the coffee and having a sluggish, unproductive morning.

Or, perhaps you're wondering if money spent on a house cleaner is the best use of your extra dollars. If that money is giving you more time to experience the things you wrote on your lifestyle design earlier in the book, such as being present with your family and friends, then the circulation of that money makes sense. When people buy things that are a waste, they typically do not see a return on that circulation. For example, I've wasted money on clothes that I spent a lot on and by next year the style was no longer relevant and had no value. You need to slow down and think about how circulated money is in fact getting you closer to your definition of wealth.

When clients first start working with me, they commonly lament, "Dominique, my money is all over the place!" Whether they were making $50,000 or $350,000, they didn't feel in control of what was happening and where their money was going because they weren't putting it to work. I once had a client living in San Francisco, working at Google, and making $250,000 a year . . . but he only had $1,000 saved. When we started working together, he kept saying that despite his high income, he felt like he had no control over his money and that his finances were a mess. Each time he got paid, he would deal with his bills and then spend the rest of his money on partying, traveling, and eating out at the city's hot new restaurants. Then he'd look up and see his bank account was about to go negative. So we made a plan to begin circulating his money by putting his money to work in investments and into his health instead. No longer would his dollars be free to run around doing whatever they wanted, but would instead be put to work in service of what was actually important to my client and how he viewed a life of wealth.

You can figure out if you're spending or circulating by asking yourself a few questions:

First, **is spending this money going to bring about any kind of return?** The item I'm purchasing should provide emotional or monetary value to my life beyond instant gratification. It needs to have an ROI, or return on investment, even if that ROI isn't an exact dollar amount. Pause to consider the return:

- Is this money that will just be spent or will it provide a return on investment (ROI)?
- What will the ROI be?
- How soon will I see a ROI?

Maybe you're thinking, *Okay, but buying clothes brings me joy.* The question is, will the joy be temporary or long-term? Most new clothes (and purchases of objects) provide temporary joy unless it's a lifelong piece. I want you to ask yourself: *How long will this provide me joy?* If you will only enjoy the item for a few months, then you haven't created a meaningful return.

Second, **is spending this money providing value to my life, someone else's life, or the community?** If people's lives are positively impacted by that money being spent, then it's likely you're circulating it. This can include the donations you give, the people you hire, or the small businesses you patronize. By spending your money with them, you're essentially saying *thank you* for the service or products they're providing to you.

Third, **is this purchase getting me closer to my wealth goals or further away?** If an expense is getting you closer to a goal that will help you make more money later on, it's being circulated. A good example of this is purchasing a course or educational item that allows you to learn a new skill. The money you're spending at a language center down the street is not only getting circulated into the community; it may also help you learn a second language and therefore be more marketable when you look for a new job. Once you understand the concept of circulation, you can plan out specific jobs for your money. Think about employees in a company: everyone has a role. Let's run through some of the roles your money can play.

- **Head of Housing.** The job of these dollars is to put a roof over your head. Traditional financial advice will tell you not to spend more than 30 percent of your income on a mortgage or rent, but in reality, this will vary wildly depending on where you live and your other expenses. I believe the *max* someone should be paying for housing is 40 percent of their income, but that only works if your other expenses are low. Decide what percentage of your dollars will be in circulation here and if that amount feels good to you based on what you're trying to achieve for your life.

- **Head of Keeping the Lights On.** Many of your dollars should be hard at work for your utilities. From electricity, to gas, to trash, these dollars are keeping you safe so you can do your best work, connect with your loved ones, and get a good night's rest.
- **Head of Nutrition.** These dollars are keeping you and loved ones well fed. From the money you spend on groceries to the money you spend treating yourself, look at these dollars hard at work keeping your belly full.
- **Head of Uniforms.** Whether you need a new work outfit, or some new running shorts, these dollars are keeping you clothed. If they help you stay confident and motivated during whatever requires your attention that day or week, they're doing their job. If they're tempting you into fancy shoes that you'll never wear but cost a fortune, they're probably not.
- **Head of Fun.** Fun looks different for everyone, but these dollars know that their job is to decide what that is for you. Don't look at fun as wasted money. With the mindset of circulation in play, this is money spent keeping your spirits high, giving to your community of artists and entertainers and business owners, and giving you back the energy you need.
- **Head of Transportation.** These dollars are hard at work getting you to and from work, your kids to and from school, and all of you over to visit friends and family. These are essentials that keep you connected to your work and your city.
- **Head of Protection.** We'll talk about the exact protections you need in a later chapter, but this role is all about keeping you healthy and safe. From health insurance to doctor visits to investing in your overall wellness, this money should be hard at work safeguarding the very best version of you.
- **Head of Future Planning.** Some of your money should be working toward the life you'll lead decades from now, ensuring

you have a great place to retire. This is not just money set aside; this is money hard at work creating a future that you'll enjoy.

- **Head of Legacy.** Most of us put our money to work for more people than just ourselves. Look at this money job as the one leaving an impact for you, whether it's on those close to you or those you'll never meet. From estate building to wealth transfers to donations, this money should be hard at work leaving a legacy for when you're gone. **Are your dollars doing their jobs?**

Most of us have been through a work performance review at some point in our lives. Some of you might even deliver the reviews. These are important moments because they provide a good gut check on how we're performing at our jobs. The same process is important in knowing if your dollars are doing their jobs. While thinking about your money in this way might be new, constantly reviewing your plan is key. Here are four questions to ask for each money job to understand if your dollars are doing precisely what you want them to:

- Is this money being circulated?
- Are these dollars bringing back the right amount of return?
- Are any of these dollars being wasted?
- What dollars need to be reallocated so I'm getting the right return?

For example, one of my students who lived in San Francisco decided not to have a car. Her "Head of Transportation" dollars went exclusively to Uber and bus rides, which had a $550 monthly allocation. However, when she reviewed her spending one month, she had spent $872, and the month before that, she had spent $798. On top of the exceeded budget, my client was often late for work because her Uber canceled or wasn't available, and sometimes she had to rent a car for a long-distance adventure. Eventually she realized that between the stress caused by showing up to places late, and the annoyance of dealing with car rentals, her transportation dollars weren't doing their job. It would make more sense and save her money to allocate those funds to owning a car.

I recently went through a similar assessment in evaluating my "Head of Child Care." My nanny costs for my two children are substantially higher than putting my girls in school, and a school would give me more hours of coverage. My "Head of Child Care" money is no longer serving me by paying a nanny and these funds would be better spent at a school.

This is how you assess the job that your dollars are doing.

Ask yourself: Are your funds doing their jobs to meet your needs *right now*, or do they need to shift?

Your review of each money job should include whether the money is being efficient and returning as much value as you're putting into it. Is any area underperforming? Have you been putting too many dollars to work in one area and not enough to work in another? Being in charge of your money requires keeping an eye on how your dollars are being circulated and what value they're bringing back your way. This is how you circulate your way to wealth. It's a simple decision that has a huge impact.

CHAPTER 8

Turn Time into Cash

MAKE TIME INTO MONEY WITH THE THREE E'S

- Evaluate how many income streams you have.
- Explore the types of dream income streams that exist.
- Envision your own dream income stream.

Time is finite.

In recent years, I've strived to create more time for myself no matter what's going on in the world or in my life—through delegation, automation, and passive income streams. But here's my hot take on passive income: there's no such thing. I know we call certain income streams passive, and they can be mostly so. But really, they're just less involved income streams. So how do you make money when you're limited by the amount of time you actually have to work? And what if you can't work at all, like when I was postpartum and my then-partner was sick? If you're trading hours for dollars, there are only so many hours you can stay awake to work. Therefore, it's important to figure out ways to produce income that doesn't require your time—or at least all of your time—and that doesn't have to end if you can't physically work.

I've had supertalented clients over the years who were hairstylists and lawyers and artists who couldn't make money if they couldn't go to work. Plain and simple. If they got into a car accident and were in the hospital, they couldn't make a single dime. None of us wants to be in that situation. I know there are safeguards in place, like disability and paid time off and such, but net-net, if you're physically unable to work, your income will likely be reduced. Thinking about how to turn your time into cash will prevent your money flow from completely stopping in the event of an emergency.

The extremely grim pandemic experience I shared earlier was no picnic, but money was *still coming in* even while I couldn't work. Luckily, I'd been focusing on many of the things I'm about to lay out for you in this chapter. For example, back in the day, I hosted four to five live webinars a month that would bring leads into my Wealth Demystified Course. I couldn't sell the course if I didn't show up for all of these live webinars. Now, most months I only do one live webinar, but we still run them four to five times a month because we record them! This strategy produces the same sales or even more sales than I would get if I physically showed up every time. This is an example of turning your time into cash.

Even if you have a full-time job, multiple streams of income are important. Let's say you work a full-time job with paid time off (PTO) or disability time that you can access, and you think one income stream is enough because these benefits bring in money even when you're not working. I encourage people to have multiple streams of income over and beyond their full-time job because you can lose that income stream at any time if there's a reorg in the company or a change in leadership or change in priorities. Anything can happen, so having money working for you other than your job is key.

The more money you can earn without having to trade hours for dollars, the more wealth you'll be able to create. The first time this dawned on me, I was working with clients one-on-one, building out their financial plans and personally helping them create new financial goals. Person by person. Budget by budget. Hour by hour. I was a one-woman wealth-building service. I knew I had to figure out how to work with more than one client at a time, which was when I built my first program, the Finances Demystified Bootcamp.

I took the time to record myself and package my genius so the program could sell itself. I incorporated the foundational building blocks of financial planning into a single experience for those who couldn't afford my one-on-one services. I was suddenly able to work with hundreds of people every month, which I'd never have been able to do if I was trading hours for dollars. Once I had a team, we scaled the course further to hundreds of thousands of students. Today the Finances Demystified Bootcamp generates significant income without my doing anything live. I would never be able to make that kind of revenue from financial planning basics if I was teaching people one-on-one.

Eventually this same philosophy took hold with my public speaking, too. I *love* live experiences. Being in a room teaching people how to build wealth is one of my favorite things. But back in the day, speaking engagements were a huge tax on my time. Not only did I have to pack up all my stuff and travel for twelve hours, but I had to get everything in my life in order to be gone for three days while I was only being paid for part of that. Now that I've moved my speaking engagements virtual, I can make tens of thousands of dollars for a single hour, and I don't have to travel, pack, sleep in a hotel, or take on any of the burdens of being away from my home and kids. If I'm seventy years old and someone wants to hear me speak, I can just hop on my computer, do my talk, and make some money. I've shifted this stream of income from being 98 percent in-person gigs to 25 percent in-person gigs, which is my ideal breakdown so I still get the occasional energy of an in-person room (because there's nothing that compares to that vibe).

Let's look at an example that might apply to you. Say you're working as a high school English teacher. You could create an account on Fiverr, a freelancing platform, and provide copyediting services to companies, making half your monthly salary in one-twentieth of the time it takes you to be a teacher. You could then use that money to create a course on how to self-edit your own writing, something that every communications professional or person self-publishing a book might be interested in. Once you get accustomed to working in this way, the time commitments get lower and the money you bring in gets higher.

Turning your time into cash is about more than just making money. It's also about protecting yourself from the chaos of the future. As we've seen in the last few years, *anything* can happen. Whether you're running your own business or employed by someone else, jobs can end. Even if you have unlimited PTO, if you leave your job, that benefit doesn't go with you. I don't know about you, but I don't want to work forever. If you want to retire at some point, or even if you don't want to retire at all, you probably want to get to the point where you can work less, right? No matter what you decide to do in the years ahead, I want you to feel like you *made* that decision rather than feeling like you had to. Multiple income streams can prepare you for any contingency.

Evaluate How Many Streams You Have

Streams of income include full-time jobs, part-time jobs, side hustles, investments, passive income, etc., and some people say that the average wealthy person has seven. I don't know who came up with this number or why. Seven may sound good, but I'm more concerned about the quality of the streams. You could have two really great streams and that would be enough. You could have eighteen crappy income streams and barely be getting by.

To build wealth, you should always have your eye on your main revenue stream. This is known as your main position. Having a solid main position creates stability in your life, and that stability gives you financial confidence and the freedom to think about extra income streams. If you haven't built a consistent income stream for yourself, it's hard to think about anything else. I've been there and this state of mind absolutely drains you. I thought it might be helpful to lay out my current income streams, or where all my money is coming from and how many hours I spend in each area.

- First, I have the Finances Demystified program, which is my primary income stream or main position. I make the majority of my money from this business, but it's also the majority of my time and expenses. This program accounts for about 75 percent of my time and 80 percent of my income.
- My speaking engagements are a second stream. I do both virtual and in-person events at a high hourly fee. This accounts for about 10 percent of my time and 1 percent of my income.
- My brand deals represent a third income stream. I partner with major corporations to talk about important financial issues or products. This accounts for 8 percent of my time and 6 percent of my income.
- My trucking company is a fourth stream. I'll share more about this income stream in detail later, but it's almost entirely passive. It accounts for 0 percent of my time and 1 percent of my income.
- Affiliate payments is a fifth stream. I get paid when my audience clicks or buys something I'm passionate about. This requires 1 percent of my time and accounts for 1 percent of my income.
- This book is a sixth stream. I was paid to write it and will earn more money from it as more people buy it. This book requires 5 percent of my time and will result in 1 percent of my income over a year.
- My investments are a seventh stream. I spend a lot of time here because I love nothing more than to nerd out on trading and

investing. If I took my passion hours out of it, investment would only take up about 1 percent of my time and would result in 15 percent of my total income.

It turns out I am your average wealthy person with seven income streams after all! But this number will vary based on your individual circumstances. Seven streams, in my opinion, is a lot for most people, and as I said, your focus should be on quality over quantity. I have certain streams that I expect to bring in $100,000 a year. Some may bring in less, but if the stream only brings in $150 a month, I'm not doing it. I get that for some people $150 is a game changer, but for me, it's not enough. It doesn't make sense based on my time.

To responsibly turn time into cash, you have to know how much time you're putting into things. When I worked with clients one-on-one, I asked one about her income streams.

"I have my day job," she said.

"Cool."

"And then I do Uber."

"Okay, how many hours a week do you put into Uber?"

"Twenty-five."

"All right, that's a lot of hours."

"Then, I do hair for twenty hours on the side."

I then had her assess what she was actually making from each job, so we could understand how much money she was actually taking home. Despite working really hard, she only earned a couple hundred bucks on Uber. Then she was doing hair but losing a ton of time in the car driving to people's houses. So I gave her ways to think about minimizing the time spent—such as having clients come to her—thus lifting the overall hourly rate.

Let's say the client stopped doing Uber and went all in on doing hair. She would need to understand if this strategy was going to produce more money total. If so, it would benefit her to cut out Uber completely because it's better to have two high-quality income streams than three that are spreading you superthin.

A new income stream won't appear out of thin air. It requires work on the front end. But if you're putting a ton of time in with no end in sight, you're setting yourself up to be tired and stay tired, potentially without the return or the enjoyment. I think about when I started my first course. I was putting in tons and tons of hours. But I knew that eventually, the time I'd spend on the course would be minimal, and the income would be high, so it was worth it. The operative word is *minimal*. I sometimes see people making the mistake of setting up a new income stream and thinking they'll never have to lift a finger for it ever again. For income streams to continue to produce really good results, they do require some ongoing maintenance. Passive income is never 100 percent passive. It's just less involved.

This is obviously going to vary dramatically due to each individual situation, but it's important to begin thinking about your streams of income and how much time each one is actually taking you. When I look at my speaking engagements, right now those take up about five hours of my time a month in total, but they bring in $25,000 at least. That's worth it. My brand deals don't take a ton of time, either, but they also bring in five figures a month. If those two streams took up fifty hours respectively, those same numbers wouldn't be worth it to me because it would detract from other income streams.

Let's look at a few examples of income streams that get "less involved" over time. As a personal trainer, you might need to spend a year or two driving to other people's houses to build your business. Then you could have them come to you and raise your prices. After that, you could add group Zoom classes where many people work out at once from the comfort of their homes. Your time investment would go down but you'd be making more money.

I knew a young woman who started baking cakes, and over time, her designs improved and she was able to increase her prices. But then she realized that she was only able to make as much money as the hours that she could bake. So she decided to create a less involved income stream teaching people how to decorate cakes and then earned money from her cakes *and* her courses rather than just the cakes themselves. Taking her plan further, she used that extra income to hire someone to help prep at her bakery. This gave her more time to market her business and build other revenue streams, like selling her famous icing in jars, making her even more money without having to trade her time for her hours.

If you're wondering about the difference between a "less involved" income stream and a side hustle, the answer is in the *hustle*. With side hustles, the hours you need to make meaningful money don't decrease over time. The amount of time you need to put into Uber driving at the beginning of the job is roughly the same amount of time you have to put in for the same amount of money two years later. On the other hand, the amount of time you put into a digital product is high at first, and then the time needed for the same amount of money two years later is way less, helping you turn time into cash.

The single question you can ask to determine if something is a side hustle or a less involved income stream is this: In one year, **can I make significantly more money in significantly less time?**

Let's see how this plays out: Uber . . . no. Organizing people's closets . . . no. Cutting hair . . . no. Landscaping . . . probably not. You get the drift. Look, there is absolutely nothing wrong with a side hustle. It's a great way to make extra income and provides an additional stream. But you want to spend your time, like your money, wisely. If you're getting minimal return for your effort, you will feel squeezed, stressed-out, and tired—all feelings that probably weren't anywhere in your lifestyle design. Because you only have so much time in a day.

Types of Dream (Income) Streams

Take a walk through any major city and you'll be inundated with different income streams: Ubers, car sharing, real estate, room sharing, you name it. I'd like to spend this section introducing a few types of income streams you can consider. But first I want to note that while I'm a huge supporter of education and have aspects of my business that teach people important financial skills, you could buy every top-notch course out there and still not make a dime. You have to actually *do* the work.

To this point, I once knew a woman who attended every one of my events and all the high-priced entrepreneurial conferences, too. She talked a good game about starting a career counseling business, but years went by, and as far as I knew, she never actually made any money despite numerous "investments" in making money.

Recently I saw this woman at another event and she told me, "Dominique, you were right from the beginning. I needed to just hit go and start something." Now she's making a couple hundred thousand dollars a year from her new income stream, providing career coaching and guidance to people who are transitioning jobs or looking to increase their salaries. Once she was willing to do the work to make her new income stream a reality, this woman could put all her education to good use.

With that in mind, let's take a look at some income streams I think have great potential.

Digital Products

Time Commitment: High at first, low after six months
Financial Commitment: Low

Your expertise can be turned into a digital course that helps people to learn and grow. A successful course requires having an audience, and once you build it, you can pull different levers to get people to come.

(They don't just come on their own, though. I wish; that would be dope.) A digital course requires a start-up investment. Even though this amount can be small, say a couple hundred dollars, you must also be prepared to invest time. You must create your curriculum, make videos, create the content, and set it up on a platform.

My favorite software to use is Kajabi, which allows you to do everything including course setup, coupon codes, newsletters, and websites. It's an all-in-one tool with different pricing tiers depending on your needs and audience size. The ongoing costs for digital courses include marketing budgets to keep enough eyeballs on your course that people eventually buy.

Amazon Stores
Time Commitment: Low
Financial Commitment: Low

Having a physical store requires a massive investment in time and resources. Having an Amazon store requires less. If you can carve out a need in the market on Amazon—let's say one-time-use, lavender-scented, heated eye masks—there's a way to make consistent and ongoing money within the Amazon ecosystem.

Drop Shipping
Time Commitment: Low
Financial Commitment: Low

If you're awesome at creating lit graphic tees, drop shipping could be calling your name. This income stream involves creating products on places like Shopify where you add your designs and partner with a drop-shipping company to do everything else: printing, packaging, and shipping. This stream requires driving an audience to your product, which will likely require both up-front investment and an ongoing marketing budget. However, if you can get the numbers to work in your favor, you can produce a consistent income stream.

Car Sharing
Time Commitment: Low
Financial Commitment: Medium

If you have a car you're not using very much, it might make sense to make it available to other people to drive. This would hopefully offset your car payments, insurance, and gas, and ultimately make you money. There are interesting tools like Turo and Getaround that don't require you to do much other than approve the rental and keep your car clean and up-to-date. These services are often hyperlocalized, so research what's available in your city to determine if this could be a steady income stream that requires minimal time.

House Sharing
Time Commitment: Medium
Financial Commitment: Medium

Have you ever considered renting your house while you're away for an extended period of time? Or renting out a guest room that you never use? Making money from your existing physical assets can be a good move depending on your situation. There are plenty of platforms that facilitate house sharing globally, like Vrbo and Airbnb, but there are local companies who manage it, too.

Real Estate
Time Commitment: Medium
Financial Commitment: High

In many markets, buying a home and leasing it to renters can be a great way to make almost-passive income. Not only are you covering your mortgage with rent, but you're making money over and beyond that. Obviously this requires an up-front investment of purchasing the home, and requires fees and time associated with maintaining the home and supporting the renters. If you don't mind being someone's landlord, this could be an option for you.

The previously mentioned business ideas could be qualified as less involved, meaning that they don't require an abundance of time or money to start or maintain. But by no means are they the only ideas out there, and sometimes the ideas that are most "out there" end up being the most lucrative.

My trucking income stream is a perfect example. During the pandemic, I noticed that with deliveries skyrocketing and e-commerce exploding, trucking was in demand. I had a friend with a company called Passive Trucking who educated me about how to get started in this booming business. The breakdown looks something like this:

First you have to find and buy the truck for around $50,000. You can lease it or pay cash. Then the trucking management company takes over, and you earn about $4,000 a week per truck. So you pay the $50,000 and then benefit from the value of the eighteen-wheeler truck, which typically increases or holds its value (unlike cars). So, you could sell that truck in three years and get the $50,000 back if you needed, while having made $144,000 over those same three years. Let's say you're doing this with up to five trucks; that's $240,000 a year, which is a salary. This is the type of income stream that has very little involvement. Aside from doing all of your research, contracts, and planning up front, after that it's basically passive income.

I share this example because most people don't go looking for these "less involved" income streams, especially if they're off the beaten path.

They don't even know this whole passive trucking concept is a thing. And it's not a slam dunk. You have to have the money to buy the truck (or the credit to finance it), a truck driver to partner with, and then the right approvals. Most people aren't set up financially to have this in place, which is why our previous chapters are so important. By having made great wealth decisions, you open yourself up to even more rock-star income stream possibilities. Most people (myself included) wouldn't even know to google "passive income" or "truck management," but now you do!

Envision Your Dream Stream

Before I started my first online course, I knew exactly how much money I needed to get it started, how many students I would need to earn my money back, and my goals for the number of learners each month. I had an initial plan. Unfortunately, I see far too many people trying to ride the tails of the next hot income stream, maybe something they saw on TikTok or Instagram, without having a plan or understanding of what it will take right now and in the future to get that income stream to rock.

Any time you start an investment of your time and energy, you need to know what the time line is on your ROI, or return on investment. Because hoping and praying that investing money will turn into an income stream isn't how it works! Even with the truck, I knew if I paid $50,000 now, once the truck got on the road, I'd be getting an immediate return of $4,000 a month. I would pay off that investment in just 12.5 months. Today I'm looking at buying a business. When I project when the return will happen, I expect to have my money back by the end of June.

I've seen people put a ton of money into something and then give themselves three months to make it work, without having asked themselves any of the right questions up front. I once knew a seamstress, Kate, who wanted to sell her patterns to other people learning how to sew. She put a lot of work into creating these patterns and sending them out, but she didn't realize how expensive and time-consuming that process would be and never thought about how many customers she would need to make a profit. Without a plan, Kate had no idea what to expect.

DREAM UP YOUR OWN! Now, get out a pen and think through how to create your dream income stream:

What idea do I have for a possible income stream?

_____

_____

How much money does this income stream require to get up and going?

_____

_____

When will this income stream start generating money?

_____

_____

How confident am I that the timing will work out the way I expect?

_____

_____

What is the expected time line for getting a return on my investment (as in, making my money back)?

_____

_____

If that time line were doubled, would I still be able to make this investment?

_____

_____

> If I did not make any money on this income stream or if I lost money on it, would I be putting my family's livelihood at a huge risk?
>
> _____
>
> _____

Words to the Wise

If someone tries to tell you that you can become a millionaire instantly with some hot new income stream, you should probably run. That's just not how income streams work. When something *does* start making you money immediately, it likely requires a significant up-front investment that most people can't afford (like buying $100,000 worth of eighteen-wheelers). These are the most common mistakes I see people making when trying to get a new income stream up and running:

Striking Gold Overnight

There's no such thing as overnight money with a new income stream. If there were, everyone would be doing it. Be incredibly discerning of things you see online especially. Every income stream worth having is going to require a bit of research, time, and investment in order to get going.

Audience Building Is Real

They say content is queen, because that's how you build an audience and get your business to sell. You have to play the content game if you're trying digital products or drop shipping. This means being poppin' with your social media game and newsletters. It will even mean getting familiar with social media ads. Audience building is no joke, but once you learn how to do it, you can get those online sales going.

Having a solid content plan is key. Your plan should include setting a schedule of when you will post, automating your posts, determining what type of content is performing best, and then making changes to your content based on how people are responding. The main thing is to be consistent and provide value! I see a lot of people spending a ton of time on a digital business without thinking about the audience they'll need to earn consistent money.

Think About How to *Sell*

Some people create online stores and get stuck with tens of thousands of dollars' worth of product. Not enough business owners think about how to *sell*. They waste a ton of time on the product because they gave no thought to the marketing side of things. Shoot, I sold my investing course before I'd ever built it! Spend some time creating your first email list by gathering addresses in your contacts or warming up an old list that you haven't communicated with in a while. Think about ways you can reach your target audience. Will you do in-person events? Will you collaborate with like-minded people who have an audience that might want what you're selling? Will you do a free online class where you pitch your product at the end?

Give It Time

Your new income stream will take time to earn out. You need to know exactly how much time so that you can adjust your tactics and understand what's working and what's not. I see plenty of individuals not giving their income streams enough time to work out. I also see the flip side, or people who spend too much time before they make a change or iterate on their strategy. You want to find the sweet spot in the middle.

Don't End Up Naked

Occasionally you need a quick infusion of cash to make something work. This isn't the same thing as a consistent income stream that generates money month over month. I've witnessed people deciding to sell everything they own in order to have another stream of income. They go from a perfectly lovely living situation to barely having any furniture to sit on or clothes to wear because they've sold it all. These quick cash infusions can be great for getting what you need to start your new dream stream, but they're not a stream themselves. Eventually you'll have nothing else to sell and you'll be sitting naked on some boxes in your living room.

Your time is one of the most valuable wealth-building assets that you have. The more you can make each hour worth, the closer you'll be to a position of greater financial confidence. There are so many ways to do this. What has worked for me may not work for you. However, I encourage you to continue thinking about the ways "less involved" income streams can be a part of your overall wealth-building plan so that your time is worth far more tomorrow than it was yesterday. Just remember to always keep that one income stream or main position steady and stable while you build others on top of it.

CHAPTER 9

Use Money to Make Money

FIVE STEPS FOR MAKING MONEY WITH MONEY

- Familiarize yourself with investment types.
- Consider your risk profile.
- Invest in what you know.
- Think about retirement right now.
- Be open-minded about nontraditional ways of making money.

was sixteen when I taught myself how to invest. All those years
helping my mom write her checks had translated to a real intrigue
around money and how it worked. So, aside from picking up every
Black Enterprise and *Wall Street Journal* I could get my hands on, I
decided I wanted to learn even more. I went to my family and asked
if they knew anything about investing. Everyone just looked at one
another and then back at me.

Eventually my grandfather piped up and told me about his investments. He said that he didn't know much about how the investment in his government Thrift Savings Plan (TSP) worked, but
I could take the prospectuses (documentation required by the US

Securities and Exchange Commission for all publicly traded companies) and see what I could figure out. I remember looking at his TSP and seeing basic funds like a C fund, which is common stock; a G fund, which is a government fund; an I fund, which is an international fund; an F fund, which is a fixed fund; and an S fund, which is a small-cap fund (*small-cap* means companies with a smaller market capitalization). I researched these different funds to understand the investments made and how they operated.

I labored over these documents, and my grandfather bought me *Investing for Dummies*, which I devoured alongside Investopedia, a website that is the "encyclopedia of investing." If this were happening today, I probably would have been down a crazy rabbit hole on YouTube watching investment videos. I thought I wanted to become a stockbroker because I loved the speed at which stock markets operated. I geeked out on how to analyze various investments, and I was fascinated by how money can make more money. Until then, I just thought you earn money and then spend it, and then earn more money. I didn't realize that money was a tool for making more money. I opened my first investment account and purchased fractional shares in two companies that I really loved. With $25, my first two investments were in Apple and Jones Soda, because I loved my iPod and my green-apple flavor soda. After those initial investments, I opened an E-Trade account and a Roth IRA, which is an individual retirement account (IRA) that is tax-free (meaning you do not need to pay taxes on the money that is earned from the investments in this account) and easy to run by yourself.

When it came time to find a college internship, I knew I wanted to find one at a financial institution, but no one looked like me. Where were the stockbrokers who were Black women? Then, while flipping through a magazine, I finally found Mellody Hobson, who worked at Ariel Investments, and Carla Harris, who worked at Morgan Stanley. I decided right then and there that I had to work for Morgan Stanley, too. Unfortunately, at the time I was in college, only banks and crappy internships were recruiting at my historically Black college, Bowie State University, but I wanted to be in New York for the summer because it was the epicenter of finance.

I discovered a program called the University of Dreams, which paired student interns with elite financial institutions for a hefty fee to the students. When I got accepted, I put together a proposal convincing my mom and grandpa to fund a program in which I had to *pay* to go to New York to work for free. Any adult in the room can see how that sounds crazy, but I wouldn't back down. I laid out the pros and cons, pieced together the money, interviewed with a few companies that recruited from the program, and got picked by . . . *Morgan Stanley*. My dream had come true.

Right before I was about to start, I was notified that Morgan Stanley cut their entire summer internship program. I was devastated, but eventually the University of Dreams program placed me with UBS instead. I started my summer working sixty-hour weeks behind the scenes on any task that the financial planners needed. I helped with opening new accounts, and my biggest project was supporting a new financial advisor who had recently moved to the firm. We migrated all of his clients over to UBS, an operational feat. I was getting hands-on experience in the stock market. I determined that this was in fact the direction I wanted to go in professionally . . . except, nobody there looked like me except the administrative assistants.

During this internship at UBS, I saw things I'd never seen in my life—financial accounts with two commas. I stared at the astronomical amount of money sitting in these accounts and thought, *Oh my god. This is insane. People actually have this much money.* That summer exposed me to what was possible.

Luckily, I was sitting in the meetings where clients and advisors strategized about how to make their money work for them through investing. These accounts were gaining hundreds of thousands of dollars per year with little to no work. Most of these wealthy people had had portfolios for twenty or thirty years and they all understood the golden principle to wealth: you have to invest money to make money.

Wealth building requires investing. Just working a job will not, most likely, build wealth. Just working a job won't provide for a comfortable retirement, either. Investing can even get you out of debt more quickly! I'm excited to break down everything you need to know to begin investing and building wealth.

Let's say you're twenty-five and you're maxing out your 401(k) (which is great) and your company is matching your contributions (even better). By the time you get to retirement, your tax bracket could be over 50 percent. You'll only get half the amount of money out of your retirement account one day, which is why just putting money into one isn't enough to retire. For example, let's say you save $1 million for retirement, but you haven't paid taxes yet. The tax rate is 50 percent. That means that if you were anticipating having $1 million in retirement, you'll only have $500,000 after you pay taxes. It ain't gonna work. You've got to play a new strategy by having multiple things working for you—like 401(k)s, Roth IRAs, and other types of investments.

Investing, while not a flip of a switch, will make your money work for you. When you invest, you're putting money into something that will pay you back plus a return at a later date. Given that context, let's break down the types of investments that we'll be talking about throughout this chapter and beyond. An important note, though—there's no point spending your precious time going into the weeds on these investment types. I'm sharing enough basics for this chapter to make sense. Otherwise, you'd have a textbook in your hands and nobody wants that!

Stocks

A stock is essentially a share of ownership in a public company. *Stocks* and *shares* are synonymous. They are also called *equity positions*. You can purchase one share, multiple shares, or fractions of shares. When you're buying a stock, you're buying a piece of the company. If a company is trading at $120 a share, it's going to cost you $120 to own that one share. You make money from stocks in two ways: a) when the stock price goes up and increases in value, and b) when the company declares a dividend and it is a dividend-paying company. Stocks can be invested in the long term when you hold them for a return, but when you look for a return in the short term—it's called trading.

You might be wondering where stocks are traded and how they get their value, and that's where the stock market comes in. The stock market is where publicly traded companies are bought and sold via physical or electronic transactions on the exchanges. The two main exchanges you'll hear about the most are the New York Stock Exchange (NYSE) and Nasdaq.

The largest securities exchange in the world is the New York Stock Exchange, which is a publicly traded company. More than nine million corporate stocks and securities are traded on the NYSE in a single day.[1] The difference between stocks and securities is that securities can be other investments that aren't stocks, such as mutual funds, exchange-traded fund (ETF) bonds, and options.

Next you have Nasdaq, another large exchange where all the trades are electronic. It is the second-largest stock and securities exchange in the world. It typically attracts more tech and growth-oriented businesses than the other exchanges. So, some people consider NYSE old-school while Nasdaq is younger and hipper. This doesn't matter at all when it comes to your investments, of course, but it's the brand recognition each of the exchanges seems to have at the moment.

- **Pros:** Stocks have high return potential if you invest long term, and some stocks are eligible for dividend payments, if offered. (Well-established companies that don't need to reinvest profits back into their own business may share profits with stockholders using dividends.) So, if you're looking for income, this can be a great way to go. Additionally, it's rather easy to follow the performance of one company.
- **Cons:** There's higher risk. If the company you've invested in fails or has bad performance, you could lose all of your investment.

Bonds

Bonds are complex because there are just so many of them. But the main thing to know is that bonds are essentially debts. When you own a bond, it's turning you into a lender. You are giving money to a company. Different companies take your money to do different things. Whatever they're using it for—to build a bridge or grow a company—they will pay you back the principal (the original amount of money) plus interest. That payback will vary based on how the bond is structured, what the interest payments look like, etc.

Bonds are considered to be a more conservative investment because you'll recoup your principal investment plus interest. Bonds are rated grades AAA through D, based on the financial strength and ability of that borrower to pay you back the principal and interest on time. Lower-quality bonds, also known as junk bonds, might pay you back higher interest rates, but there's also a higher probability that the borrower may default and you might not get your money back.

- **Pros:** Bonds are considered a less risky investment and can provide consistent income and a preservation of capital. They can protect some of the assets in your portfolio from risk. Retirees or someone approaching retirement is a good fit for this investment.

- **Cons:** They have lower returns and low-grade bonds can default.

Mutual Funds

Mutual funds allow you to buy hundreds, sometimes even thousands of stocks all within one fund. I like to think of a mutual fund as an Easter basket. During Easter, as a kid, you get a basket with all kinds of different candy: Apple, Google, Amazon, Tesla, Starbucks. They're all candy inside a mutual fund. The cool thing about mutual funds is you can choose which ones you want to own by what interests you. They could all be tech companies in a tech mutual fund. Or you could have a socially responsible mutual fund with all B Corporations. Or you could have a marijuana mutual fund with only companies in that space. Or you could do something more general, like the Growth Fund of America, which is one of the largest mutual funds in the country and has hundreds of top companies on the S&P 500 (which measures the value of the stocks of the five hundred largest corporations by market capitalization listed on the NYSE or Nasdaq[2]). Look for mutual funds that have companies you want to invest in or have an industry you want to invest in (for example, tech mutual fund, retail mutual fund, energy, etc.). One thing to note about mutual funds is that they trade at the end of the day at 4 p.m. EST, when the market closes. The net asset value of a mutual fund is determined based on the closing price.

- **Pros:** Mutual funds are run by a fund manager, so it's set it and forget it. You can decrease your risk here, as you are invested in hundreds, sometime thousands, of companies, instead of just one. You're paying a low price to invest in numerous companies and they have more regulatory oversight.

- **Cons:** There is a lower return potential due to the decreased risk. Mutual funds only allow one transaction per day and often have higher management fees.

Exchange-Traded Funds (ETFs)

ETFs, which are index mutual funds, closely track the performance of specific indexes (such as the popular S&P 500). The S&P 500, which is short for the Standard & Poor's 500, is a stock market index that tracks the stock performance of the five hundred large companies listed on stock exchanges. ETFs were first launched in the US in the 1990s, and advancements in technology allowed this particular investment to be passive for individual investors. Fees vary and are typically higher than mutual funds because there is a lot more work involved to calculate and trade. Returns on ETFs are typically a bit lower than mutual funds because people hold them for a much shorter time.

- **Pros:** This is a set-it-and-forget-it investment. You don't need to monitor it closely since it's managed by a professional fund manager, and its returns will be close to those of the specific index it's tracking, such as the S&P 500. Your risk is spread out among hundreds to thousands of companies, so it has a lower risk than just investing in one company. Because ETFs are traded on exchanges similar to shares of stock, they tend to be more cost-effective and liquid.
- **Cons:** You have less earning potential/lower returns due to the lower overall risk and exposure. Also, the investment management fees can be high.

Consider Your Risk Profile

Not everyone will invest the same amount of money in the same type of investments. The reason there's no one-size-fits-all approach to investing is that people have different appetites for financial risk. You might be superconservative with your money because that makes you comfortable. Or you could be superaggressive at heart, but you need to play it conservative because of your circumstances. This would have perfectly described me when I was broke. It wasn't until I was out of debt, with my emergency fund back in place, that I was able to be the risky investor I'd always been.

We all have a risk/reward profile, which is the technical title given by a financial institution where you open an investment account. After you answer a few questions with whomever you're opening a brokerage account, you are scored from low risk to high risk and given one of five profiles—conservative, moderately conservative, moderately aggressive, aggressive, and very aggressive. The latter profiles are the higher-risk ones, and the former profiles are the lower-risk ones. During times in my life when I had a conservative profile, it was because I couldn't handle the risk of losing money.

This risk profile doesn't dictate other areas of your life, though. For example, you've heard me talk about the kind of saver I am. I'm obsessed with that rainy-day fund being far bigger than anything I'd advise someone else to have. This technically describes the financial profile of someone with low risk, because instead of having a year of emergency funds, I feel comfortable with five years of funds. However, when it comes to my investments, I want all the risk. That's what I like. So, not all risk is the same. An investment risk/reward profile is related to just that—investments.

Let's talk about conservative investing versus aggressive investing. Those in the conservative risk/reward profile don't like any risk. They don't like any movements in their money like you'd see in the stock market. They want to keep their money and would rather it grow less if it means that they can guarantee it'll all still be there.

Moderately conservative to aggressive people—or those in the middle—invest in things like mutual funds, high-interest bonds, real estate, and large- to small-cap stocks. If a stock is large-cap, that just means the company has a large market capitalization—the total value of all the publicly traded shares of that company. So, a large-cap stock would be stock in a company like Apple or Amazon. Large-cap companies are considered less risky than small-cap companies because they're more established. Riskier investments tend to swing in value—going low, going high, going back low again. If you want to learn about these riskier investments, I encourage it.

When we get into high risk/reward profiles, we're normally talking about investments that are trading things like binary options and futures, highly speculative penny stocks, or high-value collectibles or art. You don't need to know too many specifics about these riskier investments, but I mention them so you'll have some exposure to what they are.

People who want to invest with lower risk are going to (typically) be similar to those who hoard their money. They put their money under their mattress (or in a savings account with very little interest) and would rather that money not compound into something greater than risk losing even a dollar of it. People in the middle-risk profiles want to invest, but don't want to risk too much. They want to be in the market and they want to make money but they don't want to see their money go down too much. People with higher risk are down to put it all on green and see what happens.

When you're investing, it's important to find balance. You don't want to put all of your money in one asset class because then you can either lose it all in one scenario or hardly grow it at all in another. You don't want all of your eggs in one basket, no matter how high you are on the risk/reward profile. Everyone should be thinking about how they can balance their appetite for risk and a proper return. If you're working with a certified financial planner on an investment portfolio—which I'd recommend—that person can help you determine the right percentages of stocks and bonds depending on where you're at in your wealth-building journey.

Let's say you have a high risk/reward profile, so your breakdown is 80 percent stocks and 20 percent bonds. If you had a much lower risk/reward profile, it might be the opposite. If you're within ten years of retirement, you shouldn't be taking on tons of risk since you don't have enough time to rebound from major losses.

Remember, if you're not creating a return, you're not building wealth. That's the entire point. If you didn't need a balanced investment strategy, I would just tell you to take your money to the nearest casino. But that's not our goal. Our goal is to invest money to make money, which requires knowledge and strategy.

Invest in What You Know

When people want to start investing, I encourage them to choose a few investments in things that they know. I always recommend the same three places to start: something you use every day, something you love, and something that's fun. Let's say you live in Texas and want to invest in the energy company that you use there—NRG in Houston would be your first investment. Something you love might be Starbucks coffee, so you'd make that your second investment. Maybe something fun is a new clothing rental company you adore, so that might be the third.

Now, there is a reason these three buckets exist. When you know and use something every day, you typically understand what a company delivers on, what their products are like, and what might be coming down the pipeline.

When I first invested in Apple, I did so because I loved the iPod. Something about the innovation and simplicity of that device captivated me. I remember the days when I had to lug around the Walkman and a few cassette tapes if I wanted to listen to more than one artist. That was followed by the days of having a trunk full of CDs. When the iPod came out, I thought it was one of the greatest inventions ever: thousands of sounds in this handy, little device. My appreciation for those features eventually extended to all of Apple's devices—easy to use, beautiful to look at, and a cult following with huge revenue potential. I continue to invest in Apple because I'm involved, which means not only do I love and use everything they make, but I keep close tabs on what's coming out, right? I have a good eye on upcoming innovation.

This kind of investment strategy makes learning fun. When I'm in Starbucks and I'm drinking my Caramel Macchiato, I feel like I'm sitting in my own coffee shop that I partially own. Because I love the company and also own its stock, I'm invested in its success. When investing is just another job or task, it becomes like homework. You don't want to do it as much. So, this is a way to be intentional about how you're choosing things and setting yourself up to stay engaged.

It also makes the research part easier, which you're (sadly) not off the hook for. And without further ado, it's time to do some investment homework. In the following four steps—also included as a downloadable worksheet—you'll do some fundamental and technical analysis around companies you might consider investing in so you're making good choices before putting your money in.

Step 1: To begin choosing your investments wisely, make a list of all the companies you use in your day-to-day life, from your grocery store to your car insurance. Try to think of at least five to seven companies. Write them all down, as there's no right or wrong here.

Step 2: Research different aspects of these companies. Go straight to Google, type in the company's name or their stock symbol, and see what comes up across results and news. You're looking for information about what's going on in their business, trying to understand the value of what you're buying and if there are opportunities to invest while a company might be discounted. This will give you a return when the market eventually reflects the company's fundamentals.

Knowing the intrinsic value of the company is considered fundamental analysis. Write down three things you find out about each company: for example, a new executive hire, a product update, a management change, cash flow, balance sheets, a recall, or anything positive or negative you read in publicly available documents. The goal is to understand if the market is accurately reflecting the company's value at the time you're investing.

For example, if you were looking at Amazon at the time Jeff Bezos stepped down, that would be an important note because it directly impacted the health of the business, lowering the value of the company in the short term. This would make it a good time to invest because the rest of the company's progression over a five-year period would show that it's in a good spot. When you look at Amazon on the chart over the last five years, it has trended upward. This makes sense, because if you were to read the news on Amazon, you'd know that the company is increasing product lines, venturing into new sectors, and is on track to keep growing. You can tell these fundamentals by following headlines about the company.

Step 3: Now you'll do something called technical analysis. Look at the chart of a company's stock value across fifty-two weeks (or beyond that) within the website or app that you're using to invest—once you select a company there will be a button to open up this chart. Take note of the week highs and the week lows. If the current value seems low compared to last year, this might be a great time to invest. This is very high-level technical analysis, which is okay. When you're investing in something like Starbucks, for example, you're keeping your money there for years, not weeks. As you're looking at the value of the company's stock, you don't need to time your participation exactly; you just want to make sure you're joining the party at a time that's logical and fair.

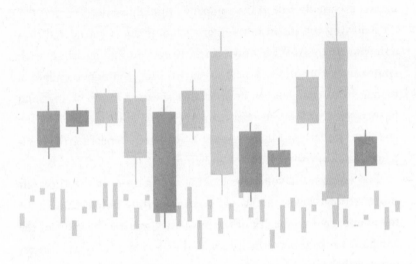

Step 4: With this fundamental and technical analysis in place, you can feel confident in investing your money. Choose three companies and pick a set amount to invest each month based on what you have available per your magic numbers. Divide that amount into these three stocks, automate your payments with your investment platform of choice, and build and grow your portfolio. My favorite platforms to do this vary. Right now I use E-Trade, Robinhood, Webull, and Trade-Station, but this will surely change. To see the most up-to-date list of the platforms I prefer and my analysis of each, refer to information at the QR code in this book.

Repeat this process anytime that you want to add investments to your portfolio. And remember, just like savings, automate your investments so money is added or invested in these accounts on a regular schedule.

Retirement Is a Right-Now Thing

Whether retirement feels like a lifetime away or right around the corner, I want you to be armed with the right information when it comes to your investments. I've seen too many people make incorrect assumptions that left them with far less money in their twilight years than was comfortable or planned.

When I was working at the financial advisory firm United Capital, which is now owned by Goldman Sachs, we had a bunch of clients who were Marriott executives. One was thrilled to spend the next few decades traveling the world with his wife. They were going to do it all—Italy, Japan, Antarctica. It was something they'd saved for, to the tune of millions of dollars in retirement. There was just one catch: all of his money was in pretax retirement accounts, meaning that because of his $400,000 annual income bracket, this money would be taxed at over 50 percent. So, he didn't have the two million dollars he thought he did. He had less than half that. When I told him, he was in tears. He hadn't realized that all of that money would be taxed because he came to a financial planner late in life and had never been educated. That's not just miscalculated money; that's years of his life when he'll either have to go back and work or won't be able to afford his living and care. It's a valuable lesson that you shouldn't only have money in taxable retirement accounts; it should be diversified across many types of investment and savings accounts.

Retirement accounts are broken into two types. In one type, such as a 401(k), you're taxed on the money when you withdraw it. That's good news now because you can sock away money that is protected from being taxed. And if your employer provides a 401(k) matching program, you're basically getting free money. But you have to consider that if your goal is to have more wealth when you retire, you will likely be in a high tax bracket and your 401(k) will be penalized.

In the second type, such as a Roth or simplified employee pension (SEP) IRA, you pay taxes on the money up front so it isn't subjected to any taxes in the future. As of this writing, you are only allowed to put $6,000 into these types of accounts each year. The amount can change each year, based on inflation and cost of living. But if there weren't a limit, everyone would be putting in hundreds of thousands of dollars and the government can't have that.

The big question is always this: How long will your money last in retirement? How much do you need? Well, let's say you're used to living off $100,000 a year. Let's also say that in retirement, you bought a house and you're still paying that house down. You still have a car and bills. If you're only expecting to be retired for five years, $500,000 might be enough. Even if you have a million-dollar portfolio, that's ten years if you're used to and comfortable living off $100,000 a year. Keep in mind that your cost of living will definitely go up, which means that the money you set aside for retirement won't go as far. Living off $100,000 a year right now is very doable for most people, but in twenty-five years that might not be the case. Also, due to extended life expectancies, most of us retiring around age sixty-five need our money to last around thirty years.

Now you're hopefully seeing the importance of having a diversified investment portfolio to make your money work for you. Lately I've been teaching people the benefits of investing in dividend-generating portfolios, so instead of drawing down from a retirement account, the dividends generate enough money to live. Let's say you have a $500,000 portfolio with high dividend-earning stocks that generate a minimum of $50,000 a year. So now that $500,000 portfolio earns $50,000 each year, and within ten years you've doubled your money. That same portfolio is going to last you much longer!

As I've been saying throughout the book, you really want to think about your finances collectively. You have your savings, your before-tax investments, your after-tax investments, and your various risk/reward profile investments. You want to try to put as much money as possible into things that will be tax-free. While I can't give you set percentages for dollars in each account, you should always prioritize your emergency savings first, while also contributing the amount your company matches to your 401(k). Many people also like to contribute small amounts to a Roth IRA, even if it's just $10–$15 a month. This is probably the easiest way to pass on wealth tax-free.

Think about the decisions you need to make to put the right investments in place now. You don't want all of your money sitting in one location, because that's setting you up for failure. And don't wait. Even if you're still in debt, I want you to be investing. I've seen plenty of people pay their debt down more quickly because they were able to use the market to make money.

Before we close this chapter, I'd like to say a few words about "sexy" investments. You know, the type of opportunities that call out for your money. I've heard it all before—marijuana is sexy. Oil is sexy. Energy is sexy.

You know what's sexy? Investing in what you know, use, and love. When you love something and it's a major part of your life, that's what's really sexy, because you know why the company is successful. Even investing in mutual funds can be sexy because you're spreading risk and using a professional to manage your funds. Investing in only "the hot and the buzzy" tends to be very high-risk. I've seen people lose a lot of money in sexy investments that everyone was on board with, even smart and discerning investors. So use your best judgment, rather than simply following the latest investment craze.

Nontraditional Ways of Making Money

When I was studying to become a licensed financial professional, what was considered *new age* or *nontraditional* would be totally traditional now. At that time, ETFs and index funds had only been around for about ten years and people found it novel that you could manage your own investments online without a broker. Let's look at some sexy and admittedly higher-risk investments that are considered new age today, which I tell my students to be open-minded about.

Crypto, Crypto, Crypto

There are entire books on cryptocurrency, which is a form of payment that uses encryption algorithms and runs on the blockchain, or a distributed public ledger that keeps a record of all transactions. Let's take a look at how this works, as outlined by the State University of New York at Oswego's Campus Technology Services:

> The use of encryption technologies means that cryptocurrencies function both as a currency and as a virtual accounting system. To use cryptocurrencies, you need a cryptocurrency wallet. These wallets can be software that is a cloud-based service or is stored on your computer or on your mobile device. The wallets are the tool through which you store your encryption keys that confirm your identity and link to your cryptocurrency.[3]

This is the first time in history that people don't have to depend on traditional financial institutions to make financial transactions or invest. The federal government and International Monetary Fund will eventually get on board here and bring regulation to this technology.[4] Until then, this is a high-risk investment that could bring great returns . . . or not.

However, if you can handle the risk, there are huge opportunities to build wealth with crypto. This can be done by simply buying and holding crypto, trading it, or even staking it. Staking crypto is when you lock up your crypto holding to earn very high interest rates. For some people with large amounts of crypto, staking can create a whole additional stream of weekly or monthly income.

NFTs

A non-fungible token is a financial security of digital data kept on the blockchain. Because the ownership of NFTs is on this ledger, and can be transferred by the owner, NFTs can be sold and traded. You can go down some major rabbit holes on the internet and teach yourself everything you need to know (I'm no NFT expert but I do own some). At the time of this writing, NFT sales are down 98 percent, but shoot, they could be up 200 percent by the time this book is published. Who knows. That's what makes them risky. Owning an NFT not only gives you the value of that NFT, but it also acts like exclusive membership into a community built around it—essentially buying and guarding access that can be sold. The NFT I own gets me exclusive desserts at one of my favorite restaurants because it allows me access to a private menu.

Art and Collectibles

Whether you're buying a work of art because you love it or because it might have value one day, art normally is a buy-and-hold type situation. Same with collectibles—which can be anything from baseball cards to limited-edition Rolexes. While these items aren't guaranteed to hold their value as tastes change and the culture shifts (hence the riskier investment profile), the way to invest here is to do your research, purchase at a price you feel okay losing, and hold on to it.

Alternative Banking

Alternative banks such as Ally and Chime don't have a physical location. Some people pick them because of the yields they are getting

167

on their money or because they have less overhead so they pass their savings onto customers in the form of high-yield checking and savings accounts. Sometimes customers don't want to deal with a bricks-and-mortar financial institution, or they like that these banks offer temporary credit and debit cards and no overdraft or ATM fees. Alternative banks also offer new forms of tech support that can assist with fraud and other unfortunate things that can happen with your account. There are indeed a lot of benefits.

However, once you build the wealth we're working on in this book, you have to keep in mind that alternative banks don't offer high-touch customer service, or an individual who can answer questions, open up new accounts, negotiate fees, or walk you through options when you have an issue. Client services at traditional banks can be immensely helpful, and normally are provided once you have around $250,000 or more with their bank. I share this because this type of exposure is valuable, especially if you've never had it before. This is the kind of relationship that you're able to leverage for financial decisions like lines of credit to buy a house, which elevates your net worth. Many times, alternative banking institutions won't be able to support you in this way.

A Note about Trading

Trading is defined by more frequent transactions. Everything we've talked about in this investing chapter has been characterized by buying and holding assets for longer periods of time. With trading, you're holding for far shorter amounts of time, normally less than a few months, sometimes even down to a few hours. When you trade something, you're buying at a low price and attempting to sell it at a higher price.

Multiple types of securities can be traded—stocks, options, binary options, futures, ETFs, foreign currency exchange (forex), and more! I typically teach my students how to complete objective trading, which proceeds according to a defined set of rules, such as when to enter a trade.

If trading is as exciting to you as it is to me, I encourage you to spend time and look deeper. Ultimately, armed with the knowledge in this chapter, you have the foundational building blocks to use your money to make money. Wealth builds wealth, and your decisions now—even if you're not totally out of debt—can help you reach your goals faster. You don't have to be reading prospectuses at sixteen (that's why I do this for a living!). You simply need to start somewhere. This is your road map for beginning that process.

CHAPTER 10

Protect Your Wealth

THREE STEPS TO PROTECTING AND PASSING ON YOUR WEALTH
- Ensure you have the right policies in place.
- Set up what happens when you're gone.
- Have conversations with loved ones about your estate plan and theirs.

Nobody wants to end up sick and in the hospital, but like I shared . . . sometimes it happens. My pandemic hospital horror story entailed almost two weeks of my then-partner barely coming through his illness. It was one of the scariest periods of my life. The last thing that we were thinking about was money. Sure, it could get him in-home treatment and a private hospital, but money wasn't keeping him from getting sicker.

Those medical bills were whack, to the tune of about $100,000. I'm so fortunate we did have health insurance. If he hadn't had health insurance, we would have been forced to pay every last dime. Luckily, we could have afforded it—it wouldn't have felt good, but we could have afforded it. If this had happened five years ago without insurance, however, it would have set us back. When everything was said and done, we paid about $30,000 for all his treatments. This was a huge amount even *with* insurance. And that was for just two weeks of care. *Imagine if it had been two months.*

We can all have unexpected life events that can undermine everything we've worked so hard in this book to build, which is why we need protection. I've unfortunately seen many clients lose every dollar they have because of a single illness. One of my clients got cancer. Her insurance was awful and she couldn't work, so all she could do was depend on credit cards while she was fighting. You likely know someone who's been through this type of thing. We hear horror stories all the time about patients who end up in crazy debt because of medical bills, and it's why we see GoFundMe accounts set up so often.

While this is certainly an unfortunate commentary about the lack of safety nets in our society, it's the reality of the world we live in, and I want you to understand how to protect your wealth if the unthinkable happens to you. You'd hate to build a million-dollar net worth, get sick, have millions of dollars in medical bills, and lose everything because you didn't have health insurance. You're investing all this time in your financial future. I don't want one thing to come along and take it away.

I think about protection as a few things: insurance like medical, life, car, disability, homeowners and renters, and business insurance. I also think about it in legal terms like guardianship, prenups, legal documents, wills, and estate planning.

Protection is like having an umbrella. Let's say you've taken all this time to put your best outfit on. You've gotten your hair done and look like a million bucks with some gorgeous suede shoes. Then you walk outside and it's raining cats and dogs. Now your hair is destroyed, your outfit is soaking wet, and your shoes are permanently ruined. If you'd just had an umbrella, you could have protected your hair and outfit and you could have made it to the next place looking amazing. Your shoes might have taken a little hit, but you could have handled it because everything else was kept solidly together.

You want that umbrella to protect you from the ups and downs that will inevitably happen—from medical situations and deaths to accidents and divorces. While these aren't the most uplifting things to think about, considering them now will leave you and your loved ones so much better off. At least you'll remove the added financial burden if something bad does happen.

Insurance

There's insurance for everything these days. There are policies for calling off a wedding, being abducted by an alien, and even protecting a specific body part . . . including a mustache. However, there are a few key insurance policies I want you to think seriously about and acquire if you haven't already. These insurances will protect you, your family, and your wealth from life's most common and resource-depleting challenges. The insurance won't keep things from happening, of course, but it will hopefully prevent the undue burden of going broke because of them. Insurances are structured differently but they essentially all work the same way: you have a policy that insures you for a certain amount, and you pay a much smaller amount each month (known as a premium) to cover that policy.

Protecting Your Health

Health insurance is a big part of the umbrella that keeps you safe from financial ruin. If you don't have health insurance, you'll want to get it ASAP. There are many government programs and resources[1] to help you find and secure the right plan for you, but here are a few things to know: First, your premium is what you pay each month. Your copay is a fixed amount that you pay for doctors' appointments, prescriptions, and ER visits. Your deductible is the amount you're required to pay before the insurance kicks in and covers your bills. Co-insurance is how much you're required to pay after the deductible. Your out-of-pocket maximum is the most you'll pay for covered health expenses in that year. When choosing health insurance, consider what you can comfortably afford each month (the premium), and what amount you are comfortable paying in the event of an emergency (the deductible). While I'm not a health care expert who can tell you exactly what you need based on your income, lifestyle, and profession, healthcare.gov is a trusted resource with in-depth knowledge that can help you.

Visit the QR code for more resources on choosing the right health insurance plan for you.

Protecting Your Ability to Work

Let's say you're a hairdresser but you break your hand and can't work for a month or two. Disability insurance protects you by paying your regular wages while you're unable to work. That amount depends on the level of disability insurance you purchased. There are two standards of disability. *Own occupation* refers to your ability to fulfill the occupational duties you were performing when you became disabled. After twenty-four months, disability then becomes defined by your ability to perform *any occupation*, which means you need to prove you are unable to work any job to get your disability.[2] You can buy short-term and long-term disability policies, either through your job or individually. The policy that's best for you will be specific to your personal situation and needs, but I've added resources that can help you determine what's best at the QR code.

Protecting Where You Live

Whether there's a fire, a robbery, a hurricane, or an earthquake, your home is valuable. If you own your home, it's often the most valuable asset families have. If you rent your home, many of your valuables likely reside within those walls. Most mortgages will require that you have homeowners insurance, which is a policy to protect you if something happens to your home. Many landlords will also require renters insurance, which is a policy to protect your belongings in the event that something happens to the place where you're living.

Protecting Your Business

If you own and run a business, business insurance is probably a good idea. It will help protect you from risks like damages and lawsuits. If you don't have business insurance, you'll have to pay for these things out of pocket. You'll be on the hook if someone sues you or an employee gets injured on the job, or if your business incurs theft or vandalism. Many businesses are required by law to protect the people who work for them, but it depends on the business and isn't always required.

Protecting Your Assets

Divorce often divides your assets, which is why in a study of people over fifty, a divorce resulted in a 50 percent drop in wealth.[3] I know people have strong opinions about prenups, and that's totally a personal thing, I get it. But you'll want to give serious thought to how you'll protect yourself and your resources when going into a marriage (or even a relationship) and what you'll do if you need to end one. I've even seen people give all of their money, time, and energy to a partner's business, for example, and then when they break up, they're left with nothing. It's worth consulting an attorney to put the right legal contracts in place to protect you from splits, divorces, breakups, or breakdowns.

I've been through this before. Visit the QR code for some resources that can help.

When You're Gone

I know we don't like to think about dying. American culture is funny like that, but dying is the one thing we'll all do. Instead of acting like it won't happen, you can protect your wealth and the well-being of your loved ones by planning appropriately. The protections we'll go over in the next section are often overlooked but are wildly important for keeping everything you've built intact for your partner, your children, and even organizations you care about. You don't want your wealth to disappear into the state system if you die. You want it to go to places, people, or nonprofits that you care about.

Protect Your Loved Ones

Death can be a huge financial hit to a family. Let's say you're the breadwinner for your household and you die. What will your partner do? They won't be able to afford the house on their own because you made most of the money. On top of paying for your funeral expenses and liabilities (and dealing with grief), they might also have to move, get a new job, and make substantial cuts to their lifestyle. It's a lot to deal with, which could literally be solved if you'd had a life insurance policy that cost less than $20 a month.

I pay about $28 a month on a thirty-year term policy so that if anything happens to me, my girls will receive a million dollars in addition to the other money and assets in their trust (we'll get to that). I want each of my kids to be able to say, *Okay, my mom has passed but I'm still getting taken care of as if she's here.* Plus, I don't want my children to be a financial burden on someone else once I'm gone. That's not fair to either party, but it happens all the time. If you're accustomed to a two-income household, or if you're single and don't want people to have to grieve *and* deal with your finances, a small term-life policy can safeguard that from happening.

Life insurance exists to replace an individual's income tax-free. Your monthly payments cover you in the event that you die and your family loses you (and thus your income). Life insurance is more complicated than it used to be. You can get riders (think of these like add-ons) for children, for cancer, for nursing homes, you name it. But all that's really necessary is your basic term policy to replace the income of someone who is depended upon. You can have multiple life insurance policies, and some people do that. They might have one for their children and spouse as well as themselves. Your company might even have a life insurance policy on you if you're a key person in that business. Sometimes you'll need to disclose that you have multiple policies, what they are, and who they're for.

Make sure you get life insurance early, because in the future, you might develop an ailment that makes you uninsurable. Morbid as it sounds, life insurance policies get expensive later in life because you're closer to death. Get this when you're young and healthy. Someone who is twenty-five years old may pay $25 a month for a $1 million policy, but someone who is forty-five years old may be charged $50 a month for the same benefit.

Many people get a life insurance policy through work. If you already have one through your employer, I suggest a separate policy. That way, if you ever lose your job, you still have a life insurance policy that will take you through any and every job in your future. It's important to get these early and lock them in for the term because the earlier you get it, the cheaper it is for the decades ahead.

If you're single right now with no one depending on you, that doesn't mean you're off the hook for life insurance. It's a great idea to get a policy now, while it's cheap. You'll grow into it! I got a policy in my early twenties for a million dollars, which no one needed if I died (my mom and sister were the beneficiaries), but it was much cheaper than if I had bought it now at thirty-seven. I was thinking about my future life and what my future self would need. I've had clients say they're going to wait until they have a partner or kids or a house, but then they end up with breast cancer and can't even get life insurance.

How to determine your policy. How much life insurance you get will vary depending on your situation. But here are some helpful guardrails:

Is someone depending on me? If so, how much of my income would I need to replace and for how long in the event of my death?

Example: Let's say you have children who are fifteen years old and you want to cover them through college. If you're making $100,000 a year, you'd want to get a policy for about $500,000 to cover the five years. But if your kids are superyoung and you want to cover them for twenty years, you'd multiply your income by twenty instead of five for a $2 million policy instead. The number varies based on how you're thinking about financial coverage once you're gone.

Are there any expenses or debts that someone would be liable for in the event that I died, and how much are these? Some examples are mortgages and home equity loans, cosigners on debts, and cosigners on private student loans taken out before 2018.[4]

Who do I want to support? While life insurance is usually left to family members, I've also seen people give it all to PETA or a dog facility up the street. You can make anyone you'd like to minimize hardship for the beneficiary of your policy, whether that's your mom, kids, spouse, sister, or a nonprofit. You can even divide your policy among many beneficiaries so they all get a little something.

I have more resources for you to evaluate life insurance policies at the QR code in the back of this book.

Guardianship

If you have dependents, you'll want to be thoughtful about guardianship, which is simply a legal contract explaining who is responsible for your children should you die or become incapacitated. Setting your kids up with a financially irresponsible guardian means they can end up broke should something happen to you. If you don't have a trust and trustee in place, then guardians have control over your dollars as designated in a will, or guardianship document. For resources on appointing a guardian in the event of your death, we've got those at the QR code.

Beneficiaries

Beneficiaries are people who receive your money in the event of your passing. Beneficiaries should be set on all of your investment accounts, retirement accounts, checking accounts, life insurance policies, trusts, etc. You can set how much goes to which people, and you want to do it on every account so the money isn't tied up and causes more burden to those who are already dealing with the loss of a loved one.

Protecting the wealth you've built is critical. You cannot build the kind of wealth—money, investments, businesses, real estate—that gets passed down from generation to generation if you don't have an estate plan. *Estate planning* refers to establishing trusts, wills, transfers of money, inheritance, charity, how your money is taxed, and lots of things in between. While I'm not an estate planning attorney or expert, who is the only person you should get estate planning advice from, I do hope you recognize how important planning is to protecting your money and making sure that it goes to the right people after you die. That starts with talking about it. If I can leave you with one takeaway, it's to have conversations about everything in this chapter with the people you love.

Go Ahead and Talk about It

When I was young and being raised by my mom, she would say that if anything ever happened to her, I should go into her closet and look for a specific file box. It had every financial account, utilities account, and password we'd need to handle things so my grandparents and I didn't have to scramble to figure things out if she died. Oh, and if I looked in the inside left pocket of her red blazer, I'd also find cash.

If you've ever lost someone unexpectedly, you know how hard this part can be. Who knows where all their investment accounts were when you can't even figure out how to get into their computer . . . or their email . . . or their bank accounts? The situation can be so much more chaotic than it needs to be at a time that's already exceptionally painful. Don't expect your loved ones to know whether you banked at Wells Fargo or Chase, if you traded at E-Trade or Robinhood, or if your 401(k) was with Betterment or Fidelity. Instead, put everything in one place for them.

I want you to imagine your best friend, your partner, your parents, or a family member needing to access your life if you were to fall off the face of this earth. Now, walk through everything they'd need to know to close up shop on your life.

- How would they access your phone?
- Who should they call to let them know you're deceased? What banks need to know?
- How would they access your computer?
- What email do you use and what's the login?
- What utilities get paid and need to be shut off? How are they accessed?
- What properties exist? Are there mortgages? How are they accessed?
- What bank accounts do you have and how do they get into those?
- What investment accounts do you have and how can they access them?

- What insurance policies do you have and with whom?
- Have you paid for your funeral expenses, plots, headstone, etc.? On that note, what kind of funeral or celebration or cremation or speeches or party would you want? (Take the guesswork out of it!)

Now I want you to imagine this another way. Who could pass away unexpectedly and how can you get them to go through this exercise so that *you* aren't left with the confusion, headache, and frustrations of trying to figure out all of this on their behalf? Can you have these conversations with your parents, your partner, and your confidants? Can you encourage your best friends to do this for themselves and with *their* partners and/or family members? Nobody deserves to scramble when they're grieving, but so often that's what happens because we haven't protected our loved ones by getting this all down for them and with them.

We're reluctant to have these conversations for all sorts of reasons, but mainly it's because no one likes talking about and imagining their own death or the death of someone they love. I get it. It's not the rosiest conversation to have. And as we talked about in the beginning of this book, in many households, money is often a topic that people run from. However, *not* having these conversations makes protecting wealth even harder. Here's a way to open the conversation with friends and family members:

for you and supereasy to navigate if I'm gone. This got me thinking about your plans and wishes. Do you have life insurance or estate plans in place I should know about? Or is there anything I can do to help make that happen?"

A conversation starter for friends:
"So many celebrities do not have their estate plans in place—even though they have so much money! I've been working on my estate plans. Have you started yours yet?"

It's never too early to think about protecting your wealth, whether you feel wealthy right now or not. By considering how you will safeguard the wealth you have right now and the wealth you plan to create, you're shifting your mind into a wealthier place. When we can protect ourselves and our loved ones in the near term with things like health insurance and disability and protect ourselves and our loved ones in the long term with things like life insurance, guardianship, beneficiaries, and estate planning, we're actively choosing a wealthy life for years and decades to come.

To help prepare, fill this financial inventory worksheet in yourself or give it to family members so they know how to access your financial life in the event of an emergency. Digital versions are available at the QR code.

I Have Life Insurance With:

Insurance Company	Policy #	Death Benefit

I Have Other Insurances With:

Insurance Company	Policy #	Death Benefit

I Have Personal Property:

Property Description	Value	Other Info

My Financial Inventory

Use this worksheet to keep track of the current status of your financial life. You should use a pencil as things may change, or keep this information in a digital document. Share it with your loved ones.

I Have Bank Accounts With:

Name of Bank	Account #	Account Type
Super Cool Bank	1819191833	Personal Checking

I Have Investment Accounts With:

Investment Company	Account #	Account Type

I Have Retirement Accounts With:

Retirement Account Name	Account #	Account Type

Monthly Bill Checklist

Bill	Due Date	Amount	Jan	Feb	Mar	Apr	May	Jun	Jul	Aug	Sep	Oct	Nov	Dec
Netflix	10/22	$14.99	✓	✓	✓	☐	☐	☐	☐	☐	☐	☐	☐	☐
			☐	☐	☐	☐	☐	☐	☐	☐	☐	☐	☐	☐
			☐	☐	☐	☐	☐	☐	☐	☐	☐	☐	☐	☐
			☐	☐	☐	☐	☐	☐	☐	☐	☐	☐	☐	☐
			☐	☐	☐	☐	☐	☐	☐	☐	☐	☐	☐	☐
			☐	☐	☐	☐	☐	☐	☐	☐	☐	☐	☐	☐
			☐	☐	☐	☐	☐	☐	☐	☐	☐	☐	☐	☐
			☐	☐	☐	☐	☐	☐	☐	☐	☐	☐	☐	☐
			☐	☐	☐	☐	☐	☐	☐	☐	☐	☐	☐	☐
			☐	☐	☐	☐	☐	☐	☐	☐	☐	☐	☐	☐
			☐	☐	☐	☐	☐	☐	☐	☐	☐	☐	☐	☐
			☐	☐	☐	☐	☐	☐	☐	☐	☐	☐	☐	☐
			☐	☐	☐	☐	☐	☐	☐	☐	☐	☐	☐	☐
			☐	☐	☐	☐	☐	☐	☐	☐	☐	☐	☐	☐
			☐	☐	☐	☐	☐	☐	☐	☐	☐	☐	☐	☐
			☐	☐	☐	☐	☐	☐	☐	☐	☐	☐	☐	☐
			☐	☐	☐	☐	☐	☐	☐	☐	☐	☐	☐	☐
			☐	☐	☐	☐	☐	☐	☐	☐	☐	☐	☐	☐
			☐	☐	☐	☐	☐	☐	☐	☐	☐	☐	☐	☐
			☐	☐	☐	☐	☐	☐	☐	☐	☐	☐	☐	☐
			☐	☐	☐	☐	☐	☐	☐	☐	☐	☐	☐	☐
			☐	☐	☐	☐	☐	☐	☐	☐	☐	☐	☐	☐
			☐	☐	☐	☐	☐	☐	☐	☐	☐	☐	☐	☐

CONCLUSION

While writing the final chapter of this book, I was also writing my grandfather's eulogy—the same grandfather you've read about in these pages—the one who first handed over his retirement statements and prospectuses so I could teach myself about investing—the one who eagerly helped me get all of my debts onto the table and *decide* that nothing was too scary to talk about, that nothing could keep me from becoming wealthy—the one who bought me *Investing for Dummies*. As I wrote the words I would share at the celebration of his life, I realized I needed to also share them with you. Because as we're thinking about the final consideration in building wealth, which is determining your legacy, there's no better way to showcase what that means than to think about what someone will say about us once we're gone.

Me: Hi, Pop-Pop!
Him: Hey, Baby-O!

This may seem like a simple greeting, but these words always put a smile on my face and felt like a warm hug from the world's best grandfather.

I knew this day would come, but of course, you selfishly hope it never does.

Since the day I was born, you have been one of my biggest fans and supporters, constantly pouring your wisdom, life lessons, and confidence into me and all of your family. You showed up for us whenever we needed you. From the times you would come to my house every day after work to tutor me on topics I was struggling with (sometimes making it better, other times making me more confused), from the fact that you were one of the first people I would call if something upset me, or if my tire blew.

You'd cook pre-prepared frozen meals for me and all my college room-mates, you'd have me come to your house to go "shopping" for toilet paper and paper towels, you'd listen to me cry after life failures, and you'd moti-vate me to push forward.

We'd share trips to Indian Acres, riding around in my infamous golf cart, which you spray-painted to say Dominique's Golf Cart. We'd sit side by side as we read our Reader's Digest *and* Washington Post *and drink our black coffee, and some nights we would sneak downstairs and you would let me eat as much chocolate as I wanted (Grandma would always catch me the next morning with chocolate all over my face!). These are just a few ways you "spoiled" me, as people would say. However, the definition of spoil is to leave something alone to rot, which you never did. You just showed me tons of love!*

Now I stand here as a confident, successful two-time college graduate, CEO, mom, and leader. I impact the lives of thousands on a daily basis largely because of my Pop-Pop and the blueprint you laid out to ensure my success!

The words "thank you" are just not enough. Your legacy will live on within all of us and the people we impact just like you did.

Thank you, Pop-Pop, from your first Baby-O!

You might be wondering what words shared at a funeral have to do with building wealth, and in short . . . it's everything. Money equals freedom. Even if you say you don't want to be rich and one-percenter wealthy, everyone wants more flexibility to do what matters—to spend time with friends and family, to do things you love to do, to do whatever it is that you put on paper in your lifestyle design.

Money allowed my grandfather to have the impact I described in the sentiments above. Because he was financially secure, he could spend time with me after work, tutoring me instead of working a second job. He could buy me that golf cart, take me on trips, pay for my college, and plan fun things together that have created lasting memories that will stay with me even though he's gone. I have a lot of friends who didn't have those experiences with their grandparents because they were working so hard to provide the basics or they didn't have the financial means to travel. Money allows you the freedom to determine your legacy and have the time to create it. Because your legacy isn't something you leave on a tombstone, it's something you create with your actions each and every day.

Many chapters ago, I asked you *why you're building wealth*. I wanted you to think about what that word *wealth* meant for you personally. Now that you've taken ten steps on the path to building it, I want you to think about your greater purpose, or the impact your wealth can have. For some people that might mean donating a wing at their university, for other people that might mean having enough money to take your family on vacations, and for other people that might mean having enough money for unlimited free time with your loved ones. There's no right or wrong. You don't have to think huge (unless you want to). But you do want to define the legacy, or living purpose, that this wealth will help you create.

I've talked a bit about my grandfather's legacy already. But he also did something else. He created the financial stability to purchase a burial plot for my grandmother and himself, which left the rest of us to focus on organizing an amazing ceremony for him. Part of his legacy was ensuring he could take a few things off our plate. He took the time to impact people's lives, but also made sure to build his wealth so that we could all be in a better place, with fewer struggles than he had. My grandfather made choices every day to protect his family so his healthy financial legacy would live on.

When I'm done with this life, I want people to feel like I inspired them to decide to be wealthy and have the confidence to go do it. I want to have taught Black people, moms, and entrepreneurs how to bring their dreams to reality and I want to have taught them how to fish for themselves, even in the roughest times. If I were still broke, living out that legacy each day would be damn near impossible. Now I get to stand on a stage in front of 2,800 people, motivating them to live their most financially confident lives, and that's something I wouldn't have been able to do if I didn't push through myself.

Because this is my legacy, I can't just sit in my room and watch TV. I can't just scroll through every financial TikTok but ignore my own finances. I have to put myself out there even when I don't necessarily feel like doing so, because it's not about me. It's bigger than me.

Thinking about your legacy orders your steps. If you keep it top of mind, then you can build your life around it. Think about someone who bakes cakes. They *could* think about their business as baking cakes to make money . . . or they could think about it through a lens of purpose . . . that baking cakes is about creating love and happiness. Cakes are a part of most joyous life events—birthdays, weddings, graduations, etc. They're a symbol of happiness. Someone who bakes cakes is literally bringing the sweets that amplify a celebration, making a special day one to remember.

So, dig in and think about what your actions are *really* about. What does wealth building really mean for you in the grand scheme of things? Your actions in the moment may not seem that impactful, but if you change the way you frame them, you'll change their importance.

Determining your legacy will not only impact how you show up each day; it will also keep you focused on *your* end goal, not anyone else's. When I realized what my true path was, I stopped looking at people as competition. I'm good friends with people whom others would consider my direct competitors, but I'm so aligned with my purpose that I don't worry about that. They're going to impact the people they're supposed to impact, and I'm going to impact who I'm supposed to impact.

And look, your legacy statement can evolve. Even mine has changed over time. When I was younger, I thought I just wanted to be rich. Over the last five years, my purpose has evolved from that to impacting other women, then women of color, then moms, then Black and women CEOs. As I gain different levels of exposure and reach certain levels of success, I shift how I think about my own purpose in building wealth. I've also realized there are some things I'm no longer on fire for, like having a huge impact on the financial services industry. I've ditched the lane paved by old rich guys, and I'm making a lane for myself and all of you.

You thought about your own wealth-building goals at the very beginning of the book. Now I'd like you to return to those questions, answer them again, and create your own personal legacy statement.

- What do you want people to say about you when you're gone?

- How do you want to make people feel?

- If your day could be about creating one outcome, emotion, or benefit for people, what would it be and who are those people?

- Imagine you have the wealth you desire. What is that wealth helping you do that is in service to others?

- If you had all the time in the world to focus on one issue, one group of people that you care about, one cause, or one change, what would it be?

Use these answers to finish this sentence, which is your legacy statement:

My legacy is to (the action your wealth is helping you take) for (who will benefit from those actions).

Now write yours:

_____

_____

_____

_____

_____

_____

_____

_____

_____

_____

_____

_____

If your wealthy life today isn't what you want and dream it to be, even if it's the roughest of rough right now, remember that everything happening is all just a life experience. You are not destined to be in this place for the rest of your life. Those tough lessons are the same ones that helped me get on all those stages with a mic in hand, helped me write this book to you, helped me live my legacy at scale.

Your wealth journey has probably already presented some challenges. There's no way to make all the decisions in this book without coming up against your own fears and limiting beliefs. If you're deciding differently, it also means that you'll be making mistakes. You might even second-guess yourself. There will be times that you lose faith or forget that you ever decided to be wealthy at all. That's normal. It's part of the process.

Hopefully, though, I've armed you with decisions that will meet you where you are and guide you to the future that you deserve, one where even your wildest dreams become a living reality. By traveling through your money origins, having conversations about wealth, and tackling your personal finances—from sorting out your credit, facing your debt monster, developing a spending plan, giving your money jobs, and turning time into cash, to protecting your wealth—you have a road map to return to every time you are ready to go even further on your wealth-building journey.

You've already made the most important decision by reading this book and deciding to be wealthy. The rest of the steps will ride the momentum from that huge shift in your energy. It's an energy that will catch on and create changes that will impact you and those around you in rich ways. Your life is already more wealthy because of it and your legacy is being written as we speak, one step at a time.

ACKNOWLEDGMENTS

I am honestly still in disbelief that I am sitting here writing the acknowledgments for *my* book! This has been a dream of mine since I was a little girl, as I would sit and write mini books, create the cute covers, plop them on my bookshelf, and think to myself that one day I would have my own real book. And here it is . . . wow!

As I begin to think about everyone I want to thank, I am hoping that I don't forget anyone, as there have been so many people that been instrumental in my journey to getting this book in your hands.

First and foremost, I want to thank God. Without Him I would not be here, with this purpose, mission, brain full of ideas, and ambition. Thank You for always blessing me and being my constant go-to! God also blessed me by sending Maxie McCoy my way. For years I knew I wanted to write a book, and even had a blank Google Doc in my Google Drive titled "*New York Times* Best-Selling Book," but it was Maxie that helped me bring this dream of mine to reality. Maxie, I cannot thank you enough for asking me this simple question after you interviewed me for your podcast: "Have you ever thought of writing a book?" You saw something in me and in my story that you felt people needed to hear. Once I finally said yes, you literally held my hand through the proposal process and helped bring my voice and words to paper better than I could have ever done on my own. You then introduced me to your own literary agent, who is the best in the game, Brandi Bowles. Brandi, thank you for immediately seeing the value in my message and story wanting to help me get it out and into the world. Brandi then connected me with my dream publisher, Simon & Schuster and Simon Element. In my wildest dreams I would have never thought that I could partner with such a dynamic and iconic publishing team. Thank you to everyone at my publisher from the designers, editors, to the marketing and production teams, and a special thank-you to my editor, Doris Cooper, for championing my book and helping us to craft a message within these pages that will be easily digestible to anyone!

The stories and life experience I share in this book are all impacted and created by the loving people in my life. My mom, Beverly Welch, is one of the main reasons I fell in love with personal finance. I can't thank you enough for making money such an easy, everyday thing to discuss in our home and for supporting every single "crazy entrepreneur idea" I have ever had. To my dad, Kevin Broadway, thank you for always believing in me and encouraging my entrepreneurial energy. Bvlgari, thank you for being the world's best little sister and friend, and for always keeping me organized and helping out with the kids when I need to work or travel, and for looking up to me more than Beyoncé, lol. Your future is so bright, and I am blessed to support you the way you support me as you begin your adult life! To the world's best grandparents, John and Bernice Queen, your contributions in my life have led me to where I am today; your life lessons, examples of being great stewards of finances, and more have been beyond instrumental in my life and journey—thank you. Dion Pouncil, thank you for often seeing things in me that I could not see in myself. I could never thank you enough for the numerous contributions you have made in my life and for our beautiful children.

Marvin Welch, one of my first business partners and the best stepdad, thank you for your examples of what to do and what not to do in business. I promise to continue to make you proud and not go broke!

My children, Dawsyn and Demi, thank you for being patient as I often stayed up late or got up super early to work on this book or my other businesses. The joy you bring to my life daily is priceless, and I hope to make you proud to call me your mom.

Diana Lewis, you are the sister-friend and business partner that God knew I needed. Thank you for all that you do and for always believing and trusting in me.

I am beyond thankful for my entire Finances Demystified team. Thank you for supporting all of the many projects I often have going on at once and sticking through many awesome and difficult times within our business. I appreciate you all!

To my students, thank you all for believing in me and allowing me to be your guide on your wealth-building journey!

To all of my close friends, mentors, supporters, and followers, I can't thank you enough for constantly encouraging and supporting me.

Thank you!

NOTES

CHAPTER 1: TAKE BACK THE POWER
1. "Bankruptcy," United States Courts, https://www.uscourts.gov/services-forms/bankruptcy.

CHAPTER 2: TRACE YOUR MONEY ORIGINS
1. Kendra Cherry, "Neuroplasticity: How Experience Changes the Brain," Verywell Mind, February 18, 2022, https://www.verywellmind.com/what-is-brain-plasticity-2794886.

CHAPTER 3: GET YOUR PAST OUT OF YOUR FUTURE
1. Gail Cornwall and Juli Fraga, "Stop Venting! It Doesn't Work," Slate, March 8, 2022, https://slate.com/technology/2022/03/venting-makes-you-feel-worse-psychology-research.html.
2. Ryan C. Martin, Kelsey Ryan Coyier, Leah M. VanSistine, and Kelly L. Schroeder, "Anger on the Internet: The Perceived Value of Rant-Sites," *Cyberpsychology, Behavior, and Social Networking* 16, no. 2 (February 2013) 119–122, https://doi.org/10.1089/cyber.2012.0130.

CHAPTER 6: FACE YOUR DEBT MONSTER
1. Doug Milnes, "Average Credit Card Debt in America," MoneyGeek, October 18, 2022, https://www.moneygeek.com/credit-cards/analysis/average-credit-card-debt/.
2. "What's the Difference between a Credit Score and FICO Score?," Chase, n.d., accessed November 6, 2022, https://www.chase.com/personal/credit-cards/education/credit-score/difference-between-credit-score-and-fico-score.
3. Elka Torpey, "Education Pays, 2020," Career Outlook, US Bureau of Labor Statistics, June 2021, https://www.bls.gov/careeroutlook/2021/data-on-display/education-pays.htm.
4. Austin Frakt, "Does Your Education Level Affect Your Health?," *New York Times*, June 3, 2019, https://www.nytimes.com/2019/06/03/upshot/education-impact-health-longevity.html.

5. "The Labor Market for Recent College Graduates," Federal Reserve Bank of New York, last modified November 4, 2022, https://www.newyorkfed.org/research/college-labor-market/index.html.

6. "Fact Sheet: President Biden Announces Student Loan Relief for Borrowers Who Need It Most," The White House, August 24, 2022, https://www.whitehouse.gov/briefing-room/statements-releases/2022/08/24/fact-sheet-president-biden-announces-student-loan-relief-for-borrowers-who-need-it-most/.

7. Bennett O'Brien, "College Majors with the Highest & Lowest Unemployment Rates," HeyTutor, n.d., accessed November 6, 2022, https://heytutor.com/resources/blog/college-majors-with-the-highest-lowest-unemployment-rates/.

CHAPTER 7: MAKE SAVING SIMPLE AND SEXY, THEN CIRCULATE YOUR WAY TO WEALTH

1. "Being Financially Well Can Improve Your Health," Prudential, n.d., accessed November 6, 2022, https://www.prudential.com/financial-education/being-financially-well-can-improve-your-health.

CHAPTER 9: USE MONEY TO MAKE MONEY

1. "New York Stock Exchange (NYSE)," Corporate Finance Institute, October 19, 2022, https://corporatefinanceinstitute.com/resources/equities/new-york-stock-exchange-nyse/.

2. "What Does the S&P 500 Index Measure and How Is It Calculated?," Investopedia, October 11, 2022, https://www.investopedia.com/ask/answers/040215/what-does-sp-500-index-measure-and-how-it-calculated.asp.

3. "The Basics about Cryptocurrency," Campus Technology Services, State University of New York at Oswego, n.d., accessed November 6, 2022, https://www.oswego.edu/cts/basics-about-cryptocurrency.

4. Bilal Little and the Crypto Course on financesdemystified.com.

CHAPTER 10: PROTECT YOUR WEALTH

1. "Do You Have Health Insurance?," Substance Abuse and Mental Health Services Administration, US Department of Health and Human Services, n.d., accessed November 6, 2022, from https://www.samhsa.gov/sites/default/files/health-insurance-how-do-i-get-pay-use-with-notes.pdf.

2. "Choosing Disability Insurance: Top 10 Things to Consider," Disability Denials, January 7, 2022, https://disabilitydenials.com/long-term/choosing-disability-insurance/.

3. Ben Steverman, "Divorce Destroys Finances of Americans over 50, Studies Show," *Bloomberg*, July 19, 2019, https://www.bloomberg.com/news/articles/2019-07-19/divorce-destroys-finances-of-americans-over-50-studies-show.

4. Georgia Rose, "What Happens to Your Debts after You Die?," NerdWallet, March 24, 2022, https://www.nerdwallet.com/article/insurance/debts-after-death-life-insurance.

INDEX

ABOUT THE AUTHOR

DOMINIQUE BROADWAY is a millennial and self-made first-generation multimillionaire whose mission is to make wealth attainable for anyone. After graduating from Bowie State University and earning a master's of science in financial management at the University of Maryland, Dominique began her career working at UBS and Edelman. A self-described millennial money therapist, she walked away from her extremely wealthy clients to help everyday people. The founder of Finances Demystified (financesdemystified.com), Dominique is known for making complex financial topics simple. Her clients are often the first people in their family to build wealth, and she guides them not just through financial strategies, but also in the psychology of money so they can make the stacked decisions to become wealthy.

Dominique has been featured in *Time*, *USA Today*, Refinery29, *Forbes*, *Black Enterprise*, MarketWatch, *Ebony*, *SmartCEO*, *U.S. News & World Report*, and other media outlets.

Instagram: @DominiqueBroadway
Twitter: @MsFinanceCoach
Facebook: Dominique Broadway
YouTube: DominiqueBroadway